THE CHURCH AND HOMOSEXUALITY

A positive answer to current questions

by

MICHAEL GREEN
DAVID HOLLOWAY
DAVID WATSON

HODDER AND STOUGHTON

LONDON SYDNEY AUCKLAND TORONTO

British Library Cataloguing in Publication Data
Green, Michael, *b. 1930*
   The Church and homosexuality.
1. Homosexuality.
I. Title II. Holloway, David,
III. Watson, David Christopher Knight
261.8'34'157   BT708

ISBN 0 340 25483 1

CONTENTS

PREFACE

A WATERSHED IN THE CHURCH

Why another book on homosexuality? To many the issue is of minor significance. But the current discussion in the Church on homosexuality touches many nerves – the authority of the Bible, the value of Christian tradition, the place of the family, sex and society, law and morals, freedom and responsibility, pastoral care, discipline within the Church, and the power of Christ in the world today. In all these areas there seems to be confusion. There is a limit, however, to how long the Church can remain publicly confused, yet credible. Hence the importance of the debate.

We have written in response to a Report on *Homosexual Relationships* published by the Church of England's Board for Social Responsibility. This contains its Working Party's Report. It also contains some 'Critical Observations' by the Board. We have accepted the invitation in the Report to enter into 'widespread discussion'. It is hoped that what we have written will be of use to people who may be questioning or confused after reading the Working Party's Report. But it is also hoped that it will be of use to people who have never even heard of the Report but who may be questioning or confused as a result of the activities and publicity of the Gay Movement, including the Gay Christian Movement.

It is true that as compared with the ideas of some in the Gay Movement the Report is very moderate. Indeed it has incurred the criticism of the Gay Christian Movement for not going far enough. Nevertheless it represents a watershed. As one member of the Gay Christian Movement has said, it

9

takes the Church into the nineteen-fifties. He, of course, wants to take the Church into the gay world of the nineteen-eighties. But however minimal a 'move' and although not up to the expectations of the Gay Movement, this Report is a watershed.

The real divide is between those who argue with the Working Party that 'there are circumstances in which individuals may justifiably choose to enter into a homosexual relationship' and those who deny that. The Church over the centuries has been clear that the homosexual way is not the way of Jesus Christ. Suddenly to revise this position and fly in the face of the teaching of the Bible, as well as the teaching of the Church needs very strong argument. We believe that the arguments that favour the teaching of the Bible as commonly understood are compelling and stronger. We believe, therefore, it would be very wrong for the Church of England to endorse a number of the suggestions and conclusions of the Report.

But we must not stop with simply being negative. The Church can and should learn from the Report. There can and should be a far greater care for and acceptance of people with homosexual difficulties in the Church. It must realise too that while there is confusion at large over heterosexual morality and behaviour, it would be totally unfair to select homosexual behaviour as a 'scapegoat'.

The authors of this book have tried to put a 'positive' case. This is very difficult when you are arguing against a stated position. This was a problem felt by some members of the Board for Social Responsibility. They wanted to go further than the Board's 'Critical Observations', which follow the Working Party's Report. They did not disagree with the criticisms, but they felt that voicing criticism is not enough. In his foreword the Bishop of Truro, the chairman of the Board, said they wanted 'a reasoned and positive statement of the Church's traditional viewpoint'. But of course, 'to do this would be tantamount to writing another report'.

This is an attempt to be a little more 'positive'. Inevitably in a dialogue or discussion, there will be the 'negative', but hopefully in a creative way. Michael Green has attempted to give a general view of the subject with a look at the biblical material. I have taken time 'in dialogue' with the Working Party's Report itself, and have felt it right to go into some matters of detail. David Watson has written with pastoral issues particularly in mind. We have not been worried by reduplication of items especially as regards the biblical material. The same facts or problems handled differently can be helpful.

It needs to be underlined, of course, that the Board for Social Responsibility, as its chairman has written, 'has not adopted the Working Party's Report or endorsed its contents. Consequently publication in no way commits the Church of England or the Board to them'. Nevertheless, the Church is now faced with certain questions. We therefore offer this book as one attempt at 'a positive answer to current questions'.

I would like to thank Heather Clayton for her help in the typing of this manuscript (under pressure).

November 1979   David Holloway
                                   Jesmond Parish Church
                                   Newcastle upon Tyne

PART I

HOMOSEXUALITY AND THE CHRISTIAN – AN OVERVIEW

MICHAEL GREEN

A WORD OF THANKS

In writing this short contribution to a sensitive and controversial subject, I would like to express my indebtedness to the Report itself and the Critical Observations by the Board for Social Responsibility, which together go to make up the publication *Homosexual Relationships: a Contribution to Discussion* (CIO, 1979). I should also like to express my gratitude to the Rev David Holloway of Newcastle, the driving force behind this book, to Mr Nick Riddle, and in particular to Mr Clive Ansell, a graduate in psychology at Oxford who is a member of our St Aldate's team. Two books which I have found particularly helpful in seeking to assess and evaluate the biblical position on homosexuality are Don Williams, *The Bond that Breaks* (BIM, 1978) and Richard Lovelace, *Homosexuality and the Church* (Lamp, 1979). Both authors have been deeply involved in counselling and research in this area. Thank you, too, to Jane Holloway who retyped this against the clock on her very first morning working with me!

Michael Green
St Aldate's
Oxford

HOMOSEXUALITY AND THE CHRISTIAN

'There's nothing wrong about homosexual activity in itself. How could there be, since God gave us every part of our bodies? And provided we treat them with respect and in a life-enhancing manner, I don't feel we can go far wrong, whether we happen to be homo- or hetero-sexual. It's at this point that those of us who've had a religious upbringing, or been influenced by a religious outlook in other ways, have certain obstacles to overcome, because there is no doubt that within the Christian and Jewish traditions homosexual activity has been, and to a large extent still is, regarded as sinful.' Thus Canon Trevor Beeson in 'Thought for the Day' on Radio Four on 12 September 1979.

The modern commonsense acceptance of homosexual acts on the one hand; the dead hand of tradition and Church teaching on the other. This is the tension in the current controversy over the propriety of homosexual acts, particularly within the Christian Church and Christian ministry. Most major denominations are engaged in re-examining their attitudes to this matter, and the Church of England has recently come out with a Report which embodies the current tension with the utmost clarity. The Board for Social Responsibility commissioned a Working Party to examine and report on homosexual relationships: this they did twenty-seven meetings and five years later. And the Board who had commissioned them felt sufficiently disturbed by their Report and recommendations to publish its own critical observations within the same covers! No wonder it was eagerly awaited by the press. No wonder it caused a stir.

The Bishop of Truro, Chairman of the Board for Social

Responsibility, observes that the homosexuality issue raises questions to do with the authority of Scripture and the Church's tradition. It certainly does. If Scripture and the tradition of the Church are against homosexual activity, how much need this weigh with the modern Christian?

(a) Changing standards in sexual morality

In order to get this matter into perspective, we need to start further back. During the past few decades the Church has increasingly surrendered to the permissive spirit of the age. This is especially apparent in the field of sexual morality.

Take the question of remarriage after divorce. The early Church was rigorous on this matter, following the teaching of Jesus that whoever puts his wife away and marries another commits adultery. 'All who by human law are twice married are in the eye of our Master sinners,' wrote Justin in the second century (1 *Apol* 15), and his attitude is characteristic. Indeed, so strong was the bond between marriage partners that the early Christians had the greatest difficulty in seeing that it could be right for the surviving partner to remarry even when the spouse had died. A far cry from the present proposals in the Church of England to remarry in church divorced people whose partners are still living.

Take the question of fornication. Society says, 'Everybody does it, so why bother about chastity?' Many Church leaders condone it so long as the relationship is loving and due contraceptive precautions are taken. But this is in striking contrast to the early Christians. 'Fornication must not even be named among you, as becomes saints,' wrote Paul to the Ephesians (5:3), and in his letters to Corinth we find him excluding from the Church one who had committed fornication, until he repented. 'We who used to delight in fornication now embrace chastity alone,' wrote Justin (1 *Apol* 14), and that attitude was characteristic. There used to be a clear distinction between the Church and society in this area of extra-marital sex.

The question of abortion was equally clear-cut. The

16

pagans did it, for reasons of poverty, luxury, or simply to preserve their figure! Seneca, a contemporary of St Paul, writes of fashionable women who have abortions in order to safeguard their beauty (*ad Helviam*, 16). Plato advised that no child should be allowed to come to birth when the parents had passed the age assigned by the legislators for procreation (*Republic*, 460F). Abortion was commonplace. Paganism, like its modern counterpart, saw the foetus not as *homo*, man, nor as *infans*, a baby, but merely as *spes animantis*, the potentiality of life. Exposure of unwanted children on the mountain side and abortion of unwanted pregnancies in the womb were common expedients in the permissive society of the ancients to rid themselves of inconvenience. But Christians would have none of it. Tertullian put the position with great clarity. 'Prevention of birth [ie after conception] is a precipitation of murder: nor does it matter whether one take away a life when formed, or drive it away while forming. He is also a man who is about to be one' (*Apol* 9). Contrast that with the irresolute or condoning attitude towards abortion, as common in Church circles as in secular ones today. Remember the million foetuses aborted in the UK in the past decade. One cannot help being struck by the different stance between the ancient and modern Church.

The same holds good of homosexuality. The tradition of the Church is as uniform as that of the Bible. Whether you look to the Apostolic Constitutions, to Chrysostom, Augustine or the Reformers, the attitude is always the same. Homosexual acts are repudiated in no uncertain way. But in the light of a number of contemporary phenomena this, too, is under fierce debate at present. The Kinsey Report on human sexuality was believed to show that approximately twenty-five per cent of white American males have had some homosexual experience, while four per cent are exclusively homosexual. This dramatically changed the climate in the 1950's. The civil rights movement then encouraged homosexuals to 'come out'. The counter-culture of the 1960's

17

gave homosexuality a new face, and an increasing number of psychologists began to reject Freud's analysis of homosexuality as pathological, and maintained that it was the attitudes of society, not of homosexuals, which needed to be changed. In the States lesbianism has become part of the feminist revolt, and homosexual churches have emerged in most of the major cities. In comparison with the more extreme positions argued by American writers, the Church of England's Report *Homosexual Relationships* is extremely moderate. We do not find here anything like Sally Gearhart's view in *The Miracle of Lesbianism* that exclusive heterosexuality is a perversion of humanity's natural state, nor even the claim that homosexual marriages should be hallowed by the Church like heterosexual ones. The Working Party merely wishes to lower the age of consent to eighteen, maintains tentatively that in certain circumstances homosexual acts may be right, regards homosexual orientations as no barrier to ordination, and urges ordained men who are active homosexuals to offer their resignations to the Bishop – and these he may or may not accept.

Why, then, should Christians get hot under the collar about it? It is a fair question. I think there can be no doubt that traditional Christian attitudes have been far harsher on sexual sin in general and homosexuality in particular than on any other – in striking contrast to the attitude of Jesus, who was far more devastating to the religious and respectable sins of hypocrisy, pride and jealousy. It shows curious partiality that Christians on the Right have, on the whole, worried about personal sins while those on the Left have agonised over the social failures of the Church. Moreover, the very heat with which many people, Christians included, approach this subject raises questions about their own sexual attitudes and adjustment. There is no reason to raise holy hands in horror at the genital acts engaged in by homosexuals of either sex: all of them are used in heterosexual unions. Why then should anyone object on Christian grounds to the acceptance of homosexual acts among consenting adults as a perfectly normal alternative to the man–woman relationship in marriage?

The answer lies in Scripture. The Bible is utterly unequivocal on the matter.

(b) What does Scripture say about sex?

This is a prior question to what it says about homosexuality. Significantly, it is a question which often homosexuals, along with the Working Party, do not properly examine. And it is important. It makes no difference whether you take the early chapters of Genesis as historical or pictorial: the doctrine is the same. The two accounts of the creation of man, embodied in chapter one and chapter two respectively, make essentially the same point.

Genesis 1:26–28 runs as follows: 'Then God said, "Let us make man in our image, after our likeness; and let them have dominion over the fish of the sea, and over the birds of the air . . . and over every creeping thing that creeps on the earth." So God created man in his own image, in the image of God he created him; male and female he created them. And God blessed them, and God said to them, "Be fruitful and multiply . . ." ' Here, right at the outset of the Bible, we meet a massive repudiation of all 'Unisex' attitudes. Man is made not autonomous but in the image of God, and the plurality in mankind reflects the plurality in God. His image is displayed not in individuality alone, not in man with man or woman with woman, but in man and woman in community.

Genesis 2 is rich in pictorial language. God 'formed man of dust from the ground, and breathed into his nostrils the breath of life' (2:7). He said, 'It is not good that the man should be alone; I will make him a helper fit for him' (2:18). And he 'caused a deep sleep to fall upon the man, and while he slept took one of his ribs and closed up its place with flesh; and the rib which the Lord God had taken from the man he made into a woman and brought her to the man. Then the man said, "This at last is bone of my bones and

19

flesh of my flesh; she shall be called Woman because she was taken out of Man" ' (2:21ff). Fabulous imagery to display God's purpose of companionship, complementarity and intimacy between man and woman. All this is spoiled when together they disobey God. They find separation from one another (represented by covering their nakedness) and separation from God (represented by hiding among the trees of the Garden). From then on mankind lives in alienation, estranged in a broken world. The created order that we know, so the Bible maintains, is neither original nor final. Originally man and woman were made to reflect through their togetherness the image of God. Ultimately the redeemed will inhabit a new heaven. But today mankind lives in a fallen world. 'Nature nowhere reflects the perfect will of God,' writes Don Williams in *The Bond that Breaks* (p 57). 'The divine plan can never be established merely by observing human behaviour apart from revelation.' And it is the obstinate conviction of Christians of all backgrounds and denominations that God has revealed his will in Scripture. It is in the complementarity of the man–woman relationship that we see his will for our species. 'Therefore a man leaves his father and his mother and cleaves to his wife, and they become one flesh' as Genesis 2 concludes.

It is highly significant that this attitude is maintained throughout the Bible. To be sure there are declensions from it – polygamy, adultery, bestiality, sodomy, all are found in the lives of people in the Bible. But there is a steady insistence in its teaching that God's will for us is either marriage or celibacy. Jesus himself emphasised it in Matthew 19. He went behind Moses' concessions to the frailty of men in allowing them divorce for certain reasons and reasserted the truth of Genesis 2:24, incidentally attributing it to God himself and not merely to the author of Genesis: 'Have you not read that he who made them from the beginning, made them male and female and said, "For this reason a man shall leave his father and mother and be joined to his wife, and the two shall become one"? So they are no longer two but one. What therefore God has joined together let no man put asunder.' He followed it by offering one alternative to marriage, and one only, that of sexual abstinence. 'For there are eunuchs who have been so from birth [ie those who do not have the capacity for intercourse with the opposite sex], and there are eunuchs who have been made eunuchs by men [ie those who have been castrated, or, perhaps, those who have had no opportunity for marriage through circumstances that were no fault of their own], and there are eunuchs who have made themselves eunuchs for the sake of the kingdom of heaven. He who is able to receive this, let him receive it.'

Marriage is the exclusive, lifelong commitment of man to woman in the sight of God. This is, according to Scripture, how God intends it to be. We are to choose between marriage and abstinence. Thus homosexuality, adultery, bestiality and fornication are all explicitly and consistently repudiated throughout the Bible. All violate God's intention that man and woman should constitute one flesh in which his image is reflected.

(c) The Biblical teaching on homosexual practices

It is against this background that we must understand the Biblical teaching against homosexual practices. The prohibition, for prohibition it is, is not arbitrary. Homosexuality is wrong because it frustrates that complementarity between male and female in which the divine image is to be seen.

The Old Testament material

The actual passages which deal with homosexuality are not very numerous. The best known is the story of Sodom and Gomorrah.

The wickedness of these cities has become proverbial. It re-echoes throughout the Bible. In the New Testament alone Jesus, Paul, Peter, Jude and the author of Revelation all allude to it. What was the trouble? Well, the wickedness of the city was so great that God is represented in Genesis 18 as saying, 'I will go down to see whether they have done altogether according to the outcry that has come to me,' and there follows that marvellous passage where Abraham bargains with God like an oriental trader, gets the Lord's assurance that if there are ten righteous men in the city he will revoke its doom – and then has not the nerve to see if he can go for a lower number! Chapter nineteen shows what happened when God's angels came in human form to stay with Lot in Sodom. 'But before they lay down, the men of the city, the men of Sodom, both young and old, all the people to the last man, surrounded the house; and they called to Lot, "Where are the men who came to you tonight? Bring them out to us that we may know them." Lot went out of the door to the men, shut the door after him, and said, "I beg you, my brothers, do not act so wickedly. Behold, I have two daughters who have not known man; let me bring them out to you, and do to them as you please; only do nothing to these men, for they have come under the shelter of my roof." '

Sodom's wickedness was not exclusively homosexual behaviour. Jeremiah 23:14 mentions lying and adultery, Ezekiel 16:49 speaks of pride, surfeit of food and neglect of the poor, while Isaiah 1:9; 3:8, 9 instance their speech and deeds which 'are against the Lord, defying his glorious presence'. But the passage is perfectly explicit in abhorring homosexual practice. The men of Sodom were attempting homosexual rape. 'Bring them out to us that we may know them' is as plainly sexual as Genesis 4:1 'Now Adam knew Eve and she conceived . . .' To deny this, as Sherwin Bailey does, is sheer evasion. The men of Sodom did not merely want to know the credentials of the visitors. They wanted sex with them, and Lot averted this breach of hospitality by the dubious expedient of offering them his own daughters 'who had not known man . . . Do to them what you please'. Naturally, this fact has led Scanzoni and Mollenkott (in *Is the Homosexual My Neighbour?*) to maintain that the men of Sodom were perverted heterosexuals rather than homosexuals: otherwise the daughters of Lot would have held no attractions for them. But this argument is unimpressive. A good many more than Kinsey's four per cent will have been exclusively homosexual and practising in that climate, and the rest were bisexual, seeking their thrills wherever they could find them. We are specifically told that 'the men of Sodom ... to the last man' surrounded the house of Lot in quest for these visitors. The sexual promiscuity of Sodom had reached cesspool proportions. Not ten righteous people could be found in Sodom, and it perished. It remains a warning to men and nations. A similar story in Judges 19 reflects afresh the horror that such sexual depravity (heterosexual and homosexual alike) held for Israel, and the threat it constituted to her national life. 'There was no king in Israel; every man did what was right in his own eyes' (Judges 21:25).

If you want to find the same point embedded not in a story but in straightforward prohibitions, turn to Leviticus 18:22 and 20:13. It is part of the calling of God to his people Israel to be holy as he is holy (Leviticus 19:2). Thus 'you shall not lie with a male as with a woman; it is an abomination. And you shall not lie with any beast and defile yourself with it, neither shall any woman give herself to a beast to lie with it: it is perversion.' Such acts as the Report admits 'are part of what it means to be a heathen'. Just so. They are a repudiation of the man-woman relationship which God ordained. That is why they are prohibited.

The New Testament Material
When we come to the New Testament we find that there is no variation on the Genesis injunction of one man one woman as God's plan for sexuality. As we have seen, Jesus enjoins this or celibacy (Matthew 19:1–12) when invited to adjudicate between divorce for major or minor reasons. He goes behind the Mosaic permission and regulation of divorce 'for the hardness of men's hearts' to the original plan of God in Genesis 2:24, to which we have already

23

drawn attention. This is not to say that divorce cannot happen, but that it is the will of God that it should not happen. If that holds for divorce it certainly holds for homosexuality. Sexual expression is meant to cement the bond between one man and one woman throughout their lives; it is in this that the 'image of God' can be seen; and departures from this, be they homosexual or heterosexual, are declensions from God's ideal.

Thus when we get to the Epistles, it is hardly surprising that we find precisely the same perspective. Much attention has been drawn to Romans 1, where Paul enumerates homosexual actions, for male and female homosexuals alike, as part of what it means to be heathen (1:24–32). As any classicist knows, homosexuality was exceedingly common in first-century society. Paul does not list homosexuality and lesbianism immediately after idolatry in Romans 1:25ff because they are worse than other sins, but because this inversion of the proper relationship between the sexes is a mark of the inversion of the proper relationship between man and God. When Paul describes these practices as 'against nature' he does not mean that they are against the instincts of the homosexuals themselves: he is well aware that 'those who do such things . . . not only do them but approve those who practise them' (1:32). No, what he means is that a wrong relation between man and God (idolatry) shows itself in a wrong relation between human beings (homosexuality,– along with the other things he mentions: strife, envy, murder, deceit, gossip, ruthlessness, pride and so forth). In that first chapter of Romans he is not isolating special sins for special treatment. He is pointing out that you cannot reject God from your individual life and your society without profoundly affecting both society and the individual. Out of touch with God, we become out of touch with each other and with ourselves. There is a terrible inevitability about it. If you do not build according to the Architect's instructions, but tear his instructions up and see if you can't do better yourself, it is not surprising when chaos results.

24

That is why in this chapter Paul is concerned to show that there are two principles at present working in God's world (see 1:17, 18). There is his *wrath*, his righteous judgement against the godlessness and resultant wickedness of men: and there is his *righteousness*, his willingness and ability to put sinful men in the right with him and with each other as they repent and allow him to judge them, to acquit them and to change them.

Romans is, of all the Epistles in the New Testament, the one which digs most deeply in the human situation and the heart of God. But it insists that we acknowledge sin as sin, even if we love it or cannot help it. He can change our desires, be they to evil gossip or homosexual activity. And he can break our inborn tendencies, even though we cannot do so ourselves. That is the gospel of salvation, of rescue. The wrath of God and the justification of God are interwoven in this passage where Paul condemns the heathen sins of Graeco-Roman society. They are equally interwoven in the next chapter where he condemns the different but equally heinous sins of the Jew. Neither idolater nor religious have any covering before God's holy sight. 'There is no distinction; since all have sinned and fall short of the glory of God.' That is the judgement we must accept if we are to find the joy of forgiveness and reinstatement, 'justified by his grace as a gift, through the redemption which is in Christ Jesus' (3:23ff).

The other references to homosexuality in the New Testament are equally clear in repudiating homosexual practices. 1 Timothy 1:8–10 shows no particular bias against sexual sins in general or against homosexual sins in particular, but joins together 'adulterers and perverts, ... slave traders and liars and perjurers – and ... whatever else is contrary to the sound doctrine that conforms to the glorious gospel of the blessed God.' (NIV). Homosexual acts are wrong: but not more so in the sight of God than perjury and fornication. Once again you have a clear standard set out: but once again no special emphasis on homosexual practice as a peculiarly repugnant sin. The balance of Scripture is neither with those who justify the gay scene nor with those who shudder at it. It reminds us that we are all sinners, and all alike need the grace of God to forgive us and change us increasingly into his image.

Jude and 2 Peter have something to say on the subject. 2 Peter 2:6–10 is fairly unambiguous about the sin of Sodom and Gomorrah, instancing their ungodliness, wickedness, licentiousness and 'lust of defiling passion' (or 'lust for the sordid' if *en epithumia miasmou* is to be taken as an objective genitive). But Jude 7 is explicit. The men of Sodom and their New Testament counterparts against whom Jude protests, 'acted immorally and indulged in unnatural lust' and they served 'as an example by undergoing a punishment of eternal fire'. This passage is clear both about the sin of Sodom and the abiding warning to believers which it presents. Once again, the emphatic rejection of homosexual acts is a distinctive characteristic of the biblical evidence.

There is one other reference to homosexual behaviour in the New Testament, and it is a marvellous one. 1 Corinthians 6:9ff reminds the readers that 'the unrighteous will not inherit the kingdom of God'. And that includes all of us. 'None is righteous, no, not one,' says Scripture. It is only by acknowledging this fact, for fact it is, and coming in repentance and faith to the Lord who will both forgive and renew, that we enter the sphere of his kingly rule. But once we are prepared to repent, whether our particular sins be robbery, greed, addiction to alcohol, bitter attacks on others – or the particular sexual sins of adultery, homosexual acts and fornication, then, like the Corinthians, we will be 'washed, sanctified, justified in the name of the Lord Jesus and by the Spirit of our God'. That is to say our human condition of fallenness, whatever form it takes, is not inevitable or immutable. What good news trembles through those words. Such were some of you! The Corinthian Church abounded in men and women who had been deep in idolatry, robbery, bitter talk, homosexual and heterosexual extra-marital liaisons. And nobody said, 'You are not good enough to be Christians.' They were washed by Christ. Equally nobody said, 'Right, you can stay the way you were.' For when in the name of Jesus a man is forgiven he is also given the responsibility to live in the way Jesus lived, and moreover he is offered 'the Spirit of our God' to set him free. There is freedom for any of us, whatever our sexual tendencies, if we will allow the Spirit of Christ to set us free.

That, then, is the essence of the biblical teaching. Homosexual activity is wrong, as fornication, adultery, bestiality are wrong, because all of them defile the 'one man-one woman – for keeps' which is both the Creator's instructions for mankind (Genesis 2:24) and the clearest embodiment we can get of the total and exclusive self-giving between Christ and his Church (Ephesians 5:21ff). It is written into creation. It is written into redemption. No Church which claims the name of Christian is at liberty to repudiate something which is central to creation and redemption. That is why Christians who take Scripture and indeed tradition seriously cannot agree that homosexual relationships are the acceptable equivalent of marriage. In taking this stand the Church may have to be out on a limb over against contemporary society. That has often been its characteristic position. But if the Church allows contemporary *mores* to condition its obedience to its own basic charter, it will cease to be the Church at all.

I found it somewhat ironic that the set Epistle for Trinity XIX, the Sunday after the publication of the Church of England's Report, should go out of its way to emphasise the difference in sexual ethic between the Church and pagan society. 'Now this I affirm and testify in the Lord, that you must no longer live as the Gentiles do, in the futility of their minds; they are darkened in their understanding, alienated from the life of God because of the ignorance that is in them, due to their hardness of heart; they have become callous and have given themselves up to licentiousness, greedy to practise every kind of uncleanness. You did not so

27

learn Christ! – assuming that you have heard about him and were taught in him, as the truth is in Jesus. Put off your old nature which belongs to your former manner of life and is corrupt through deceitful lusts, and be renewed in the spirit of your minds, and put on the new nature, created after the likeness of God in true righteousness and holiness' (Ephesians 4:17ff).

(d) Biblical standards and modern dilemmas

Granted that this is the unanimous perspective of both Scripture and tradition, a number of questions immediately flood the mind.

1 *How much should the Church and clergy be guided by this unambiguous teaching of the Bible?*

The answer is 'Very much'. The Bible is supposed to be the supreme rule and guide for Christians both in belief and behaviour. This is something no Anglican clergyman can properly deny, however little he may relish it. When he was ordained he was asked by the Bishop, 'Are you determined out of the said Scriptures to instruct the people committed to your charge? Will you then give your faithful diligence always ... to teach the people committed to your charge with all diligence to keep and observe the same? Will you be ready, with all faithful diligence, to banish and drive away all erroneous and strange doctrines contrary to God's word ... Will you be diligent to frame and fashion your own selves and your families according to the doctrine of Christ?' Relentlessly these questions follow one another from the Bishop to the candidate in the Ordination of Priests. Not unless he can answer in the affirmative will the Church of England ordain him.

Or perhaps he was ordained very recently with the new Series III ordination service. Then the Bishop charged him to 'Pray that [the Holy Spirit] will enlarge and enlighten your understanding of the Scriptures, so that you may grow stronger and more mature in your ministry, as you fashion

your life and the lives of your people on the word of God.'
Just to rub the point home, the Bishop in the old and new
services is required to give him a copy of the Bible. Indeed
whenever a clergyman goes to take up a new job he has to
reiterate this biblical emphasis. The new form of Sub-
scription is less stringent than the old, but quite stringent
enough. 'The Church of England,' says the Bishop, 'is part
of the Church of God, having faith in God the Father who
through Jesus Christ our only Lord and Saviour calls us into
the fellowship of the Holy Spirit. This faith, uniquely shown
forth in the Holy Scriptures, and proclaimed in the catholic
creeds, she also shares with other Christians throughout the
world . . .' And the clergyman then has to say, 'I profess my
firm and sincere belief in the faith set forth in the Scriptures
and in the catholic creeds, and my allegiance to the doctrine
of the Church of England.' The people in the congregation
are entitled to know whether their clergyman will or will not
uphold the teachings of the Scriptures, and the issue of
homosexual relationships is a striking case in point. Scripture often goes against the opinion of the world. The Christian Church is pledged to follow Scripture.

2 *Should professed and active homosexuals be ordained?*
A clear distinction must be made there, between those of
homosexual orientation and those who are determined to
engage in homosexual genital acts.

There is no bar to a man of homosexual inclination being
ordained. Some of the most sensitive priests and ministers
unquestionably have a 'gay' disposition and unquestionably
do an outstanding work. But a distinction between disposition and acts is crucial in this, as in all other moral
areas. Temptation is not sin. Yielding to it is. And there are
many fine ministers of homosexual inclination who do not
yield to the physical temptations involved; just as there are
many heterosexually inclined who 'have made themselves
eunuchs for the Kingdom of Heaven's sake'. To suppose
that a homosexually oriented priest is unable, for example,

29

to give competent marriage counselling is as stupid as to suppose that you have to have been drunk in order to have a worthwhile opinion on alcoholism!

While, therefore, there is and should be no bar to the ordination of those who are homosexually inclined, it is totally inappropriate for someone who is determined to fly in the teeth of the Bible's clear teaching to take up or retain a position of leadership in the Church. So much is plain from even a cursory reading of some of the Church's official formularies quoted above. The Lord is willing to forgive anyone. Any Christian may slip into sin in sexual matters as in any other. But if a man is determined to go against the teaching of the Scriptures in this matter by overt homosexual acts, he is committing perjury at his ordination and every time he assents to the Articles of Religion. This is nothing less than hypocrisy, and it is inconsistent with Christianity. Ordinary people in Britain are not impressed by clergy who profess one thing and do another, and they have a deep-seated suspicion of active homosexual clergymen, which is why most of the latter are afraid to 'come out of the closet'. Perhaps the instinct of the ordinary man is sound in this matter. At all events there is one area which the Church of England must face up to. At present, if a clergyman commits adultery he is, in normal circumstances, unfrocked. But if he maintains a homosexual relationship with one or more other men he is usually undisciplined. I have heard clergymen announcing on television that they are practising homosexuals, and yet they are not debarred from officiating as clergy. Whatever the rights and wrongs of the homosexual question this is manifest inequality in the way homosexual and heterosexual deviations from marriage or celibacy are treated. This is all the more remarkable because evidence goes to show that, despite some outstanding examples of lifelong fidelity, there is considerable reluctance in the gay Christian scene to accept the restriction to one lifelong partner. It is certainly not easy for the homosexual in the present social climate to live with one partner, but it is hard to see how a *Christian* homosexual can justify short-term liaisons and promiscuity. If heterosexual infidelity is an example of being an 'open and notorious evil liver', to quote the Prayer Book, and debars one from coming to the Eucharist until it is repented of, the same must inevitably be true for homosexual infidelity. And if this is the case for the ordinary member of the congregation how can it not hold good for the clergyman?

3 *But homosexuality is natural and good!*
This is a common claim, and the Church is deemed unkind in not recognising it. If the man happens to be homosexual and acts out his urges, well, that is fine for him. But is it? My instincts may be natural but still not good. My nature is a fallen nature and it needs to be refashioned by the Spirit of God.

In point of fact it is very uncertain how 'natural' the homosexual condition is. No theories can be proved. To be sure, a 'two level theory' is at present popular with some behaviourist sex therapists, assuming as it does that *primary* homosexuals are genetically preconditioned towards forming homosexual attachments, and that *secondary* homosexuals become such in reaction against some traumatic experience of the opposite sex. This view is supposedly 'proven' by the low therapy rate among primary homosexuals, but the argument is of course entirely circular. And even if homosexuality were biologically determined, this would not mean that we should necessarily approve it. In all probability there are genetic predispositions in the case of alcoholism and schizophrenia, yet nobody argues that these are morally right, or should be encouraged and formalised in social structures. Yet the Report seems to suggest that if homosexuality were determined genetically, taking a moral attitude might be irrelevant.

4 For a Christian to repudiate homosexuality is tough and unjust

Christianity is supposed to be compassionate. Why, therefore, cannot homosexual behaviour be condoned and indeed encouraged among Christians as among other people? In the first place, because Christians are not just like other people. They are those in whom the Holy Spirit lives and whom he is conforming to the likeness of Christ. Second, because Christians see that they do not have an inalienable right to anything, even the free use of their sexuality. They do not belong to themselves. They have been bought with a price. Therefore they seek to glorify God with their bodies (1 Corinthians 6:19ff). The control of sexual urges is a possibility, and it is one we all have to exercise. It is no harder for the homosexually inclined to refrain from homosexual acts than it is for the heterosexually inclined to refrain from heterosexual acts. Or is it? Is it not the case that the heterosexual can marry and the homosexual cannot? As a matter of fact often in a community the preponderance of one sex over the other means this is not a live option. For one reason or another they are not able to marry, whether or not they have a particular vocation to celibacy. Abstinence is required of them by circumstance. That is very hard, and it requires much loving support and encouragement; but it is not impossible, as the lives of countless balanced and loving single people prove.

Indeed, let us look at this question of 'hardness' the other way round. If the direction in which this Report moves is followed, there will be three other areas of hardship opening up for Christians. First, those who have successfully fought homosexual tendencies for years may well now wonder whether their struggle was worthwhile. Moreover, there is a group, readily identifiable in clinical experience, of those who have aversion or neutrality towards the opposite sex without any corresponding homosexual tendencies. Such people have long been under pressure from 'both sides'. This Report will, in all probability, make it easier for them to be swayed by the homosexual option. And thirdly, those who have, like most of us, been through great struggles in suppressing promiscuous heterosexual tendencies, can now see the gradual erosion of the solid foundation of Christian ethics into a relativism that is dominated by the fashions of the secular world. Are these three factors not worth bearing in mind if we feel that it is hard to ask the homosexually oriented to refrain from homosexual acts? On any showing, being a Christian *is* hard and *does* call for sacrifices.

5 *Is there any hope of change?*

The answer is an unequivocal 'Yes'. There is already a forty per cent success rate in some secular treatment of this condition among those who want to change. A much higher success rate is, I believe, available to Christians who open themselves to the healing and renewing power of the Holy Spirit. It has been amply demonstrated that charismatic Christianity, as exemplified, for instance, by David Wilkerson in the USA, has been notably more successful than any form of psychotherapy or medication in setting drug addicts free. And I am confident that the same holds true in the area of homosexuality. The charismatic Christianity of Corinth saw lives dramatically transformed in this area, and the same remains true. I have seen it myself, and I possess written testimony from those who have been thus changed from homosexual to heterosexual attachment.

Such spiritual therapy will have a number of aspects. In the first place it will involve a recognition that homosexual acts are wrong and are repugnant to God, as Scripture makes plain. This leads directly to repentance, which is an essential precondition for change. And this is particularly relevant to those who do not or cannot *want* to be changed. As Philippians 2:13 puts it, 'God is at work in you both to will and to do his good pleasure.' Often when I am not willing to go his way, I tell him so, and then add, 'But I am willing to be made willing.' I invite him to work in the inner area of my will, which is just as fallen as my actions. It is his

33

responsibility to effect the change. It is our responsibility, and the essence of repentance, to allow him to do so.

Second, there will be prayer and the laying on of hands, directed towards forgiveness for homosexual actions and the inner healing of any incidents in the past which have proved formative of homosexual tendencies.

Third, fellowship is of crucial significance. Human friendship and prayer backing will be needed so as to provide support in the avoidance of homosexual encounters and stimuli, and their replacement by non-homosexual relationships.

Nor need all this diminish the life and fulfilment of the personality. Provided that the level of Christian faith is high, then, as in the case of the promiscuous heterosexual, the avoidance of a sexual encounter or sexual imagery can *in itself* be extremely rewarding and hence self-sustaining. Perhaps that is the nuance Paul had in mind when he spoke of Christians being more than conquerors through him who loves us (Romans 8:37). Not only is there the conquest of temptation, but the deepened self-realisation and relationship with the Lord Jesus Christ which results.

PART II

'HOMOSEXUAL RELATIONSHIPS' –
THE DISCUSSION CONTINUED

DAVID HOLLOWAY

1 LEARNING FROM OTHERS

'A monumental crisis is upon the Church. Avowed and practising homosexual persons demand the sanction of their lifestyles . . . I call this a crisis because it promises to disrupt congregations, shatter Church structures, throw confusion into time-honoured biblical interpretation, change the social structure of our country, and revoke our fundamental view of man as created by God as male and female.'

So wrote one church leader,[1] formerly on the staff of Hollywood (California) Presbyterian Church where he ministered to many homosexuals, and now a teacher of theology. But he was also a member of the Task Force set up in 1976 by the United Presbyterian Church of the USA to investigate the issue of the ordination of practising homosexuals. What was the significance of that Task Force? How is it significant for us now that we have been given the results of the findings of a Church of England Working Party on homosexuality?

The answer is that the Task Force (in English parlance 'Working Party') highlights certain features which seem to appear not infrequently in the Churches as they face the question of homosexuality.

There is the pressure. This is pressure from persons committed to the Gay Movement. This is all part of the background in the first place. Of significance for the Church of England in this respect was the occasion in 1977 when an Episcopalian Bishop, the Rt Rev Paul Moore, Jnr, Bishop of New York, ordained Ms Ellen Marie Barrett to the priesthood. Prior to her ordination she had been active in the Gay Movement and had served as an officer of 'Integrity', an Episcopalian homosexual group. At the time of her

37

ordination she was an avowed and practising lesbian. She claimed that 'what feeds the strength and compassion I bring to the ministry'[2] was her relationship with her lesbian partner. The Bishop justified his action by arguing, 'There is a timelessness to the message of God's love that outweighs the datedness of so many biblical injunctions, rooted in ancient societies.'[3]

Not surprisingly there was reaction. Dioceses expressed opposition at their annual conventions. The diocese of Texas asked for the removal of Bishop Moore. At Ms Barrett's ordination service Fr James Wattley said that Ms Barrett's lesbianism rendered her ordination a 'travesty and a scandal'.

The pressure in the case of the United Presbyterian Church was from William Silver. It was this that led to the setting up of the Task Force. During his senior year at the Union Theological Seminary, New York, William Silver confessed that he 'came to the point at which I could say openly that I was gay. *I told almost everyone.*'[4] He happened to tell members of Central Presbyterian Church in the Park Avenue area. This in turn led to the New York Presbytery asking the General Assembly to establish a Task Force to give 'definitive guidance' on the question of the ordination of homosexuals.

The Task Force met and produced a report for the General Assembly meeting in San Diego in May 1978. The report argued that homosexual erotic love can be good and within the plan of God. There was a minority report, however, which in contrast argued that homosexual acts are contrary to God's intention and therefore to be seen as sin. This minority report called for sensitivity towards the needs of the gay community, but not an endorsement of all that it stands for and does.

When, however, the matter was debated in San Diego, the 651 General Assembly delegates pronounced a resounding 'No' to the New Yorkers. Not only did they deny the appropriateness of homosexual ordination, but they approved a decree by a ratio of 12:1 which stated that *homosexual behaviour is always wrong*. The Church thus rejected the innovative policy of the Task Force. Furthermore, the General Assembly document declared that all sexual relations ought to occur only within heterosexual marriage. As *Time* magazine reported: 'This signals a retreat from the so-called New Morality by the denomination that published Joseph Fletcher's influential *Situation Ethics* in 1966 and four years later came close to embracing such theories officially . . . the San Diego decision will undoubtedly add to the caution in other Protestant denominations now struggling with the problem.'[5]

The United Presbyterian Church *is* influential in the USA. It is a denomination usually noted for its intellectual and academic leadership. That is why the *New York Times* also had to agree that 'The Presbyterian decision is expected to have an impact on other large liberal Protestant denominations that are undertaking discussions of the subject.'[6] In the Church of England, however, there appears to be little awareness of the discussions and decisions reached in the USA. In the Report of the Working Party set up by the Board for Social Responsibility, although it is dated July 1978, just two months after this important decision in San Diego, not only is there no reference to the General Assembly of the United Presbyterian Church, which gave 'definitive guidance' in that May, the bibliography does not include any of the literature that proved so influential.

One important parallel between the United Presbyterian Task Force and the Board for Social Responsibility's Working Party can be drawn and should be noted. It relates to this discrepancy between the findings of the Working Parties (or Task Forces) and the general mind of the Church. This has yet to be fully ascertained in the Church of England. But in so far as the General Synod's Board for Social Responsibility represents the wider Church, there is evidence from the Board's 'Critical Observations' of such a discrepancy. In the Methodist Church in the UK, which discussed homosexuality at its 1979 Conference, there was evidence of this phenomenon. What is the reason for it?

Perhaps it is because the Working Parties are not representative of the wider Church. It is true that they contain a mix of disciplines – social scientists, theologians and medical personnel. But are they representative of the spectrum of theology that exists within the Church? Certainly the Working Party of the Board for Social Responsibility can be challenged on this count. It contained *no* evangelicals at all – in itself sufficient to disqualify the Report as being an authentically 'Anglican' document, however much it may be a useful contribution from *one* element to the wider Anglican debate.

However, the results of the debate in the United Presbyterian Church following on the Task Force's report have been positive, although the report has been rejected and thus negated! The United Presbyterian Church in contrast to its Task Force's report has realised that homosexuality is related to the fallenness of God's world, and that the witness of Scripture cannot be made relative at every point. There may be some cultural conditioning in the Bible, but it is not all so conditioned. It does contain permanent and timeless truths about the nature of human existence and human functioning.

Having affirmed this, however, the Church recognised that there were genuine grounds for a change in the Church's attitude towards homosexuals. It should not change its belief about homosexual behaviour, but the way the Christian community in general responded to the homosexual was often cruel, unaccepting, unloving and homophobic. Of this, repentance was needed. Nor would this imply capitulation to homosexual propaganda. But rather it would be to take seriously the Church's ministry to those in need of help and healing, not in a superior way, but in a way that recognises that all – the heterosexual and the homosexual – have sinned, and in various ways fallen short of the glory of God. But the gospel is the offer of divine grace in

Christ to forgive, heal and 'redeem' us, in the various conditions of powerlessness and sin we find ourselves in. At times there is transformation; at other times, the promise of Christ is 'My grace is sufficient for you, for my power is made perfect in weakness' (2 Corinthians 12:9).

The Church of England as it discusses homosexuality needs to learn or relearn this as being the gospel of hope. It also needs to learn not only from the Scriptures, but also from the living tradition of other Churches at home and abroad.

It is now for the Church of England to assess the arguments of the Working Party and the arguments of its critics. My concern will be to present reasons why the Church of England should follow in the path of Presbyterians in reaffirming what many consider to be the biblical as well as the truly catholic understanding of homosexuality. We can note that Roman Catholics have recently said that those who 'judge indulgently' or even 'completely excuse homosexual relations between certain people' do so 'in opposition to the constant teaching of the Magisterium and to the moral sense of the Christian people'.[7]

NOTES

1 Don Williams, *The Bond that Breaks: Will Homosexuality split the Church* (Los Angeles: 1978) p 7
2 Letha Scanzoni and Virginia Ramey Mollenkott, *Is the Homosexual my Neighbour?* (SCM, London: 1978) p 39
3 Excerpt of Bishop Paul Moore's statement to the Episcopal Church's House of Bishops, 3 October 1977, Port St Lucia, Florida, USA
4 Report in *Time* Magazine, 5 June 1978
5 Ibid
6 *New York Times*, 23 May 1978
7 Sacred Congregation for the Doctrine of the Faith, *Declaration on certain questions concerning Sexual Ethics*, 29 December 1975

2 THE WORKING PARTY AND ITS SETTING

The 'pressure' for a Working Party to be set up by the Board for Social Responsibility of the Church of England to study 'the theological, social, pastoral and legal aspects of homosexuality' came in February 1974 from the conference of Principals of Theological Colleges. 'The Board agreed to this request and a Working Party ... was set up' (*Homosexual Relationships – A Contribution to Discussion* (CIO: 1979, p 3). References will normally be to paragraphs only.)

The Working Party
But the Working Party was set up by the Board of the first General Synod (1970–75). A new Board was appointed for the General Synod of 1975–80. The Working Party thus had been set up without reference to the Board of 1975–80. All was a *fait accompli* in terms of representation, and therefore potentially in terms of the final product.

It is of course not true that persons of academic competence employed in Working Parties are absolutely neutral. There is a naïveté in some quarters that assumes that if you set together persons of professional competence to deal with a problem that touches on presuppositions, beliefs, and, yes, prejudices, an answer will evolve that is 'objectively true'. But it is to be hoped that persons of professional competence have presuppositions and beliefs and it is to be feared that they also may have prejudices as well, sometimes masked by the very professional competence that is felt to be their asset!

What, however, were the presuppositions of this Working Party? These will become evident as we study the Report and they may become evident as we consider the Working Party's goals and methods. Let us therefore consider one of its main goals. In the Preface to the Report, the Chairman, the Bishop of Gloucester, tells us quite clearly of one of the Working Party's goals: 'No adequate consideration of homosexuality could be divorced from a consideration of sexuality as a whole.' This seems to be completely correct and a position surely all Christians would want to endorse of whatever persuasion they might be. Indeed, one of the criticism levelled against the Working Party is that they have not sufficiently followed through to this goal. Be that as it may. The fundamental question is *how* do we study human sexuality as a whole? This is where presuppositions come in. What 'authority' is going to be given to Scripture and tradition? As Christians we give primacy to the words, views and values of Jesus Christ and his apostles (Scripture). We resist an arrogant use of 'private' judgement, hence we take seriously the wisdom of the Church over the centuries (tradition). A consciousness thus develops, both with regard to what God has said and with regard to how the Holy Spirit has led the Church in understanding what God has said. A consciousness develops of 'revelation'. This is a 'given' and indispensable. It is also inescapable.

Methodology
Now, it is self-evident that Scripture is not the only 'given'; there is the world of contemporary society, which exhibits features of both pain and joy and which is examined in depth by the contemporary sciences. The Christian cannot live in a vacuum. His or her mission is to that world. But it is self-evident too, that if one believes that the findings of the contemporary sciences possess an 'inspired' quality and thus a 'final' authority, one's responses to the problems presented by homosexual behaviour will be very different to those of someone who believes that the sciences should be subordinated in matters of ethical understanding to the teaching of Jesus, the apostles and the Church. Indeed, those persons

43

would probably say that if a science claims this sort of 'authority', as a science, it is suspect.

Of course, in practice there is or should be a reciprocal relationship between God's revelation of himself and what his people see and observe of the world around them. This can work in two ways theologically. Take for example the general cluster of problems and issues that arise over the case of homosexual behaviour. On the one hand, these can be dealt with by an exercise in 'biblical theology'. This is a deductive approach, where the aim is to work out from the Bible a 'theology of homosexuality'. This can then be supplemented by an exercise in general historical theology, including, where appropriate, the confessional theology of particular Churches. At the end of the day there will be certain answers to certain problems.

On the other hand, it is possible to start and operate more inductively. Here, the contemporary sciences, or social attitudes, not only identify the problems and issues, but also provide the answer, and this answer may even be in apparent conflict with 'received tradition' and even apostolic teaching. This solution is taken seriously, but not uncritically. For an attempt is then made to see if from the Bible there can be a real validation for this 'radical' solution. If there is, then the conclusion is reached that the 'tradition', to date, was inadequate or in need of 'reforming'. It is also concluded that the apostolic teaching or biblical teaching was incorrectly understood and applied. The Church of England would claim that this has been the approach that has led to the acceptance of contraception. The Church of England would say that a proper understanding of the biblical teaching on sexuality leads to an acceptance of contraception for married couples. The 'tradition' at this point as understood by some was and is inadequate. But at no point is the primacy of God's revelation in Scripture denied.

All this, however, is a far cry from the Bishop of Gloucester, the Chairman of the Working Party. The Working Party wants to 'argue in favour of some modification of the traditional Christian position'. But its methodology with regard to the biblical material, the Bishop tells us in the Preface, was to take the 'medical facts as we now understand them to be' and then to take the Bible, but in the following way: 'We have not brushed aside what the Bible has to say about sexuality, we have indeed taken great pains to interpret it rightly. On the other hand, we have not felt bound simply to repeat its every utterance.' The Working Party has 'laid claim, under the guidance of the Holy Spirit, to a liberty of judgement in discerning what God is saying to us here and now, whether it be something old or something new'. So writes the Bishop of Gloucester in his Preface.

But what is going to be the principle of interpretation? Which utterances of Scripture are going to be repeated and which not? In the Report there is no real analysis of this 'presuppositional' problem. It is not good enough to talk about the 'guidance of the Holy Spirit' and 'liberty of judgement'. One of the functions of the Holy Spirit is to bring to mind those things Christ had and has taught his Church. Such new truth as the Holy Spirit leads us into is always an unfolding of that 'given word'; it is not something discontinuous. The Working Party, however, claims to be 'arguing in favour of some modification of the traditional Christian position'. If so, we must be presented not with the results of the 'liberty of judgement' but with arguments.

Freedom, or liberty, is a fact. We are free to make judgements as we wish. One *can* forget the primacy of God's revelation enshrined in Scripture. One need not treat it as normative or authoritative. But one then gives primacy to the contemporary human sciences, or worse still, to oneself! But if one gives these sciences a primary role, then the interpretation of the 'given' of Scripture and tradition will indeed be prejudged. 'If biology takes precedence (Kinsey), or if nature is all we have (Tripp), or if psychology and sociology must tell us about who man is (McNeill), then when we go to the Bible our principles of selectivity have already been established.'[1]

If the social sciences, medicine and psychology avoid 'absolutes', inevitably once these disciplines supply the interpreting principle with regard to the biblical text, the absolutes of the Bible will be neutralised. It is not surprising therefore to find that those areas of the Bible (and tradition) which do not fit in with aspects of current thinking are explained away. The result in the area of sexuality is not a Christian understanding of man and his relationships, but a humanistic one.

The argument that is used in support of this humanistic position goes something like this: God has made us to be truly human, and that means that our human functioning in all its aspects, including the sexual, will be fulfilled. Therefore, whatever we think brings fulfilment and satisfaction is right and the will of God.

But if we start with God, his revelation of himself and his purposes for man, a different argument will evolve. This will go something like this: God has made us for himself, and for one another. Therefore, the will of God itself is that which truly fulfils us and ensures our true humanity. His intentions determine our fulfilment. We put his will as primary. We do not put as primary what we think is our fulfilment, because we know that we can so easily deceive ourselves as to what is truly fulfilling. As we shall see, this is different to the 'personalist' type of thinking that emerges in the Working Party's Report.

A network of evil
The first chapter of the Working Party Report is entitled 'The Social Setting of Homosexuality'. It might be churlish to criticise it for being 'bland', but this is how some people find it. It is a bald statement of the way the Working Party sees things. It is this chapter that has brought some strong criticism from Professor Dunstan, a Professor of Moral and Social Theology in London University, and a member of the Board for Social Responsibility. He is concerned to speak of 'the social ills and evils' of homosexuality as well as of its

'social setting'. He refers to 'blackmail, bribery, journalistic exploitation, and worse . . . a network of evil out of all proportion to the original incident alleged, and this when the incident is no longer a criminal offence'. He says, 'the medical consequences of homosexual prostitution are grave'.

Now some would say that the answer to this 'evil' is to support and justify some homosexual activity as the Working Party does. But it cannot be as simple as that. The Gay Movement has been supporting and justifying homosexual activity, but elements of it have been exploiting and promoting some of this 'evil', or at least this was the judgement of the House of Lords in 1977, when the House refused to give a second reading to Lord Arran's 'Sexual Offences (Amendment) Bill'. This sought to lower the age of consent for homosexuals from twenty-one to eighteen. The 1967 Sexual Offences Act had legislated that 'Homosexual acts between consenting male adults cease, within certain safeguards, to be subject to legal penalties. The main safeguards were that the age of consent was deemed to be twenty-one, that coercion or prostitution in any form was banned . . .' (para 2 WPR).

However, after a thorough debate the House accepted the motion of Lord Halsbury 'that in view of the growth in activities of groups and individuals exploiting male prostitution and its attendant corruption of youth, debasement of morals and spread of venereal disease, this House declines to give the Bill a second reading'.

In the debate the 'other face' of the gay scene was painted – the 'personal adverts' of the gay publications, not only adverts for gay 'bars, hotels, motels, restaurants, houses of assignation (many of them sauna baths), but telephone numbers which lead to partners'. 'Typical feature articles in *Gay News* are entitled: How do you pick up someone you fancy? How do you solicit in a train? How to procure models – that is, prostitutes: Techniques of seducing boys: So you want to know how to do it – illustrated with line

47

drawings: Should the Campaign for Homosexual Equality continue its association with the political Left?'[2]

Now it can be countered that similar adverts and similar articles, but of a heterosexual kind, appear in the glossy 'girlie' magazines that are paraded on many bookstalls. That is true, but Christian people who take seriously the Christian sexual ethic would wish to oppose and be disassociated from such heterosexual adverts and articles because of the practices and views they represent. But if one may put it this way, there is a greater unity within the homosexual community than within the heterosexual community where the extremes are further apart. In the heterosexual community, for example, there is a radical difference, and indeed hostility, between, say, *Penthouse* magazine and Mrs Mary Whitehouse! There is no link or connection. *Penthouse* is unlikely to advertise Mrs Whitehouse's meetings, and Mrs Whitehouse is unlikely to give (intentional) publicity to *Penthouse*. But the homosexual community *is* linked, however different elements within it may be. This the Working Party admits: 'They [Christian homophile organisations] overlap considerably both in membership and in objectives with other homophile organisations' (para 12). In *Gay News* you can find information about the Gay Christian Movement and where its meetings are held. Comparable heterosexual magazines do not advertise the services at All Souls', Langham Place!

But no description of the social setting can be given without a description of the personal pain experienced by many individual homosexuals. The Working Party fails here. It is, indeed, possible to paint a picture of a homosexual couple that glows with the *claims* of joy and happiness, as they experience a relationship which has sexual expression. Here they are. They are attracted to each other; they realise they are sexual beings, and so engage in sexual activity. (Homosexual activity apparently means 'mutual masturbation, intra-crural intercourse, oral-genital intercourse and anal intercourse' (para 65).) They then continue a life together.

48

This life is both expressed in and nurtured by their sexual relationship. Norman Pittinger tells us of a couple just like this. They found, he says, 'great joy in sexually celebrating their love on Saturday night, and then kneeling side-by-side the next morning to take Holy Communion together.'[3]

That may be so. But the critic would ask questions about the quality and the permanence of that 'joy'. Ill-advised actions are not unknown to produce pleasure and feelings of happiness and well-being. The New Testament, indeed, argues that there is pleasure in sin (Hebrews 11:25), but it is only 'for a season'; they are 'fleeting pleasures'. As permanence is not usually a distinguishing feature of homosexual unions, one is then forced to ask, 'how permanent is homosexual joy?' The reality for many people of the homosexual experience is one of pain. As one psychiatrist has put it, 'The fact remains that the gay world is far from as gay as it is named.'[4] And after his extensive sociological research into homosexuality, Michael Schofield observed: 'Very few men seem to enjoy their first homosexual encounter.'[5] From my own experience, I can think of a number of homosexuals whose lives have been sad.

In the book *The Returns of Love*, Alex Davidson (a homosexual), writes of his agony and loneliness: 'Peter, can you understand it? This is the impossibility of the situation – what I may have I don't want, and what I do want I may not have. I want a friend, but more than a friend, I want a wife. But I don't want a woman.'[6]

Alex Davidson is a Christian who is convinced of the fallenness of his homosexuality and in the strength of Christ is trying to live with it and perhaps overcome it. For him it would be of no help to hear that the Working Party is wanting to lower the age of consent for homosexuals from twenty-one to eighteen, and to modify the traditional Christian position, thus allowing him and blessing a little 'Saturday night fever'. He does not want to hear from armchair sociologists that his sexual preference is a statistical norm and therefore legitimate. He knows otherwise.

49

There is nothing more cruel than to tell a sufferer that his suffering, *per se*, is good. The totality of his experience may be enriching, but those elements in it, which are evil, remain evil. That remarkably vigorous Dutchwoman, Corrie ten Boom, learnt a lot through her experiences in Ravensbruck concentration camp, as she saw her sister die along with many others and as she saw torture and hunger. But in themselves, those things remained evil.

Similarly, Paul's 'thorn in the flesh' was to be for him an opportunity for grace. But when Paul looked back on it (whatever it may have been – some think it was an eye disease) he evaluates it (in 2 Corinthians 12:7), even after the experience of the power of Christ, still as a 'messenger of Satan'. It is demonic. To say otherwise is to destroy one's vision and one's hope in God.

The doctrine of the Fall, which the Working Party really neglects, is essential to our true perception of God. It means that the world of pain and suffering, as we perceive and experience it, is not a true reflection of his character and his love. He is not a God whose intention is homosexuality.

The Christian does have a 'hope of heaven'. The lives of two of the homosexuals I have known have ended tragically. But both of these men had such a 'hope'. They knew that one day things would be better. To affirm that homosexuality is good and of God is to destroy that hope. As Alex Davidson, again, poignantly puts it: 'For me, at any rate it is an antidote against my own tormenting experience of the perversions of this world to dwell on the perfections of the next.'[7]

The Working Party as it outlines the Social Setting of Homosexuality does not emphasise, then, the 'network of evil' that some would judge to be part and parcel of the current manifestation of homosexuality in the West. For this, the Report can be criticised.

There is, however, a small reference to suffering in para 4: 'we know very little about the majority of homosexual men and women, though we suspect that many suffer considerably because they feel unable to declare their sexual preference.' If this is to suggest that it would be better if they could be publicly open about their sexual preference, or 'come out' (to use the technical phrase), that is questionable. Certain tensions would no doubt go, but is 'coming out' what is wanted? It may make subsequent change more difficult. Of course, talking with friends, pastors and doctors over personal problems is one thing. 'Coming out' is another. ' "Coming out",' writes one consultant psychiatrist who is a professing Christian, 'has similarities to the process of religious conversion, eg with "confessing the Lord". It makes a commitment to the cause ... it can be an almost conscious act of putting uncertainties away – they cannot be faced constantly – and for this reason, the homosexual is less open to change of attitude afterwards.'[8]

Social background

This section of the Report concentrates on a more general analysis of the situation as we face it today, and spells out the context in which the discussion must proceed. It does this by referring to the Report of the Wolfenden Committee of 1957, and the passing of the Sexual Offences Act 1967. 'When we consider the decade since the Act, we are able to see how some things are changing' (para 3). The Working Party then identifies all the homosexual pressure or support groups, which are known as the 'homophile organisations'. These include the Gay Christian Movement, whose 'statement of conviction' is 'that it is entirely compatible with the Christian faith not only to love another person of the same sex, but also to express that love fully in a personal sexual relationship'.

But what about the wider context? In this chapter, the Working Party draws attention to the Kinsey Report. This was published in 1948, with the title 'Sexual Behaviour in the Human Male'. (A parallel volume on women appeared in 1953.) This is crucial to the social setting of the homosexual problem. Perhaps this could have been spelt out in the Report, as could have been the phenomenon of the 'liberation' movements in the late 1960's and their influence on the homosexual movement. Few can deny that these provided a great deal of the social setting of the controversies and confusions that have developed over the question of homosexuality today.

What was so special about the Kinsey Report? It was that the data allegedly showed that homosexuality/heterosexuality was to be considered more in terms of a continuum than alternatives. The Working Party refers to a *scale* of homosexual involvement during the subject's lifetime. This reveals that for many people sexual preference is not a matter of stark alternatives, but is to be found somewhere on a continuum between an exclusive preference for sexual relationships with one's own sex, and an equally exclusive preference for sexual relationships with the opposite sex' (para 5). The Kinsey Report also argued that homosexuality was more prevalent than was previously supposed. One in twenty-four males, allegedly, were fully homosexual. Homosexuality was thus seen to be a matter of degree and not of kind and was believed to be widespread.

The findings of the Kinsey Report have been seriously challenged in terms of 'selective statistics, neurotic volunteers and the unjustifiable inclusion of early childhood same-sex experiences in proving that homosexuality is widespread'.[9] Other figures have been given. But the public mood was (and is) not concerned with the niceties of statistics. In the wake of the rejection of Judaeo-Christian views and values as providing guidelines for life, and also in the wake of the rejection of Freudian psychology as 'gospel' – Freud, of course, saw homosexuality as a developmental problem – here was food for thought. No longer would homosexuals feel isolated. There were a lot of them and they were not very different from other people, really. So a self-confidence began to emerge.

But this coincided with the rise of the 'liberation' movements. The student riots of 1968, the Civil Rights movement that preceded the resuscitation of troubles in Northern Ireland, and the gay movement can all properly be seen as part of a larger social phenomenon. The phenomenon is worldwide, but with national distinctives. In the UK it has been much quieter than elsewhere, but it is (or was) fundamentally a challenging of the injustices and inhumanities of a crass materialistic society, or at least that is how it was perceived to be. It is facile to call this challenge 'crypto-Marxism'. It indeed had and has associations with the Left. But it has been as much a striving for 'spiritual fulfilment' as for economic fulfilment – witness the use of drugs in the Counter Culture in the late 1960's and 1970's, and the drift of many of the young into various forms of non-Christian mysticism and, we should add, a remarkable returning in many parts of the world to the Christian Church. The emphasis of the 'liberation' movements has been pro-rights and pro-the-personal, but anti-materialism and anti-Establishment. It was this emphasis that allowed and encouraged homosexuals to say 'Gay is good'. It also has encouraged the revolutionary emphasis of movements like the Gay Liberation Front.

Church background

The Report does not mention the social setting of the homosexual question within the contemporary Church. Theologically, in many sections of the Church today, there is a loss of nerve. The Church of England produced recently through its Doctrine Commission a report entitled *Christian Believing*. Far from indicating what the Church of England believed, this report indicated how little the Church of England could be said to be believing anything. Shortly after the publication of this report, the then Chairman of the Doctrine Commission appeared to deny the deity of our Lord in association with others in the book *The Myth of God Incarnate*. True, the Commission has now been reconstituted, but that was the Doctrine Commission current at the time of the setting up of the Working Party which has produced this Report. This mood of disbelief, uncertainty and some would argue, downright 'heresy', has to be noted in any full analysis of how the Church deals or tries to deal with the theological issues relating to homosexuality.

If there are no guidelines, if 'situationalism' rules, how do you begin to know, when you are asked to validate homosexual relationships whether or not you are being like Peter, in his vision, when he was challenged to deny and go against previously held certainties. The homosexual lobby is saying that the Church is being called, like Peter, to a totally new position. Peter was told, when seeing 'all kinds of animals and reptiles and birds of the air' to kill and eat some of them. 'No, Lord; for I have never eaten anything that is common or unclean' (Acts 10:14). Subsequently, however, Peter was to see the meaning of this in God's demand to associate with the Gentiles – in the person of Cornelius. Cornelius was someone he normally would have avoided. Here Peter had to deny previously held certainties.

The Church of England did just this with regard to contraception. Like Peter, it saw that *actually* this was genuinely part of the Holy Spirit's leading and guiding. In Peter's case it was not a denial of what had gone before, it was indeed in keeping with our Lord's own commission (Acts 1:8). Of course, we need to remember that there was another occasion, an earlier one, when Peter was also challenged to deny and act against previously held certainties. It was in the Court of the High Priest. He did deny – but this time the Holy Spirit was not leading, and certainly not working in power; poor Peter then had to go out and weep bitterly.

We may guess that a difference between these two occasions was that Peter had grown in understanding as well as in confidence after this latter incident. The ability to discern the voice of God and the temptation of the evil one is a mark of Christian maturity, and it goes with genuine Christian believing. A Church which does not know what it believes is unlikely to have the gift of discernment. It will not have the

54

equipment for distinguishing between what can and what cannot be changed in terms of behaviour. It will not be able to distinguish the relative and the absolute. It will quite likely make mistakes.

Homophobia

But someone will ask: 'What about homophobia' as part of the social setting of homosexuality? The term 'homophobia' is common in the current debate, and refers to what the Report calls 'human hostility' towards homosexuality. It was George Weinberg who used the term 'homophobia' in his book *Society and the Healthy Homosexual*. As that title suggests, he believes the problem is not so much the homosexual as society that is 'perverted'. It is society that is sick and in need of changing because it cannot live with variety in human sexual experience. Weinberg, however, sees Christianity as a great culprit and a creator of homophobia. Equally, he opposes traditional psycho-analysis as reinforcing homophobia by treating homosexual persons as sick and seeking to change them to fit in with the heterosexual norms of society.

All this is contentious to say the least. It is undoubtedly true that in society there is an irrational fear of homosexuality, which leads to cruelties and a lack of love and care for the homosexual minority. Yet why is this? The manifestations of irrationality are wrong, but is the fear totally unfounded? Weinberg argues that society has set before children monogamous, heterosexual marriage, leading to children in the family as the ideal of life. Children are thus socialised and conditioned to be revolted by homosexual feelings and actions.

But supposing monogamous, heterosexual marriage is the ideal? Supposing that, as is now being asserted, early socialising influences in the developing child are vital in determining his or her sexual preference? Maybe there is a reason for that fear.

The word 'homophobia', as its synonym 'hostility', is in

danger of becoming an umbrella word to include *all* opposition to homosexuality, whether rational or irrational. The Working Party refers to the fact that 'in extreme cases there may be outbreaks of "queer-bashing"' (para 14). To this not only the Church but all men of goodwill will be opposed. But if the analysis of Douglas Plummer is true (para 20), why should there not be a rational fear or worry about an increase in homosexual behaviour? He argues that the homosexual challenges our 'classification systems', first with regard to the family and marriage, secondly with regard to gender, and thirdly with regard to sexual experience. But as these are areas essential to any given culture and the good ordering of society, we cannot simply re-adjust in these areas without being aware that we are doing something of momentous significance. Christian teaching itself affirms the crucial role in society performed by these life-maintaining factors. That is why the Bible and the Christian tradition has a great deal to say about them.

And the Church of England had better get it right! It is a fact, as the Report tells us, that the Church of England Moral Welfare Council's study of homosexuality initiated in 1952 influenced the government in appointing the Wolfenden Committee. What the Board for Social Responsibility, the successor to the Moral Welfare Council, publishes can have wide implications for the total community.

NOTES

1 Don Williams: op cit p 108
2 *Hansard*: Sexual Offences (Amendment) Bill (14 and 16), 14 June 1977
3 Quoted by Letha Scanzoni and Virginia Ramey Mollenkott, op cit p 63
4 John White, *Eros Defiled* (Inter-Varsity Press, Leicester: 1978) p 120
5 Michael Schofield, *Sociological Aspects of Homosexuality* (Longman, London: 1965) p 165

6 Alex Davidson, *The Returns of Love* (Inter-Varsity Press, Leicester: 1973) p 18
7 Ibid p 48
8 Roger Moss, *Christians and Homosexuality* (Paternoster Press, Exeter: 1977) p 14
9 see Don Williams, op cit pp 17–18

3 'ONLY A MATTER OF LEFT-HANDEDNESS'

In 1963 a group of Quakers writing about homosexuality said, 'One should no more deplore homosexuality than left-handedness.'[1] This view boldly seeks to make the homo-sexual issue turn on what appears to be a simple matter of fact. Is or is not the homosexual condition like the condition of left-handedness? We shall therefore need to discuss this question. But having done so, a further question needs to be asked. In the event of homosexuality being like left-hand-edness, does this *ipso facto* rule out moral evaluation?

The importance of this issue can easily be seen if we look at the discussion that preceded the passing of the Sexual Offences Act 1967. This is because the argument that won the acceptance of the majority of the elected representatives then in Parliament was that homosexual activity cannot be helped. It *was* like left-handedness. 'A proportion of all men are born with homosexual tendencies . . . One may feel sorry for them; they cannot help it, and it is their nature.'[2] These are the words of an MP who had taken part in the debates and admits the influence of this argument. It was believed that a person's physical make-up 'determined' his be-haviour. There was little or no choice.

It appears likely therefore that society's rules have been changed and homosexual acts between consenting males over twenty-one have been freed from the threat of the criminal law, because it was believed that homosexuals, or at least a significant proportion of them, are 'born and not made'. Their condition was due to pre-natal rather than post-natal factors. No doubt better arguments could have been brought forward for a change in the law. But this was a key argument then used. What do we say about it?

First, it needs to be noted that there has been a considerable shift in thinking in the last ten years. The Working Party itself now reflects this shift. Its arguments imply that more weight than before has to be given to the post-natal or 'nurture' period of a child's development. We cannot say that the homosexual condition is all due to inherited or genetic factors.

But what is the medical evidence for this? The medical evidence on homosexuality forms the substance of the second chapter of the Working Party's Report. This chapter is entitled 'Sex, Identity and Human Relationships – A Medical View'. But it reaches no conclusions, or rather the conclusion is that 'at present medical science can give only a very incomplete account of the formation of sexual orientation' (para 86). This is underlined later on in the Report, when we are told that 'the medical evidence is tantalisingly inconclusive' (para 218). And so it is.

It is not helped by the enormous literature that the subject of homosexuality is attracting to itself. Who can be the expert? Another problem is that there are as many different types of homosexuality as there are of people with homosexual preferences. The stereotypes need to be broken up. Great care therefore needs to be taken over applying current ideas or solutions to particular cases.

Definitions

The Working Party begins this section with 'definitions'. That is a good place to begin. But we miss here a discussion of the appropriateness of some of the terminology which is used in current homosexual debate. The Wolfenden Committee for example had thrown down the gauntlet as long ago as its Report when it said: 'Some writers on the subject, and some of our witnesses, have drawn a distinction between the "invert" and the "pervert". We have not found this distinction very useful.'[3] (An 'invert' was someone believed to be thoroughly homosexual in condition and whose condition was rarely remediable; a 'pervert' was someone capable of heterosexual responses who engaged in homosexual behaviour.) If Kinsey's 'continuum' is right, there are 'degrees' or 'levels' of homosexual 'tendencies'. Thus rigid classifications may not be always helpful.

Who then is a 'homosexual' and what is 'homosexuality'? A group of Anglican clergy and doctors wrote in 1954 just prior to the setting up of the Wolfenden Committee: 'It is most important to understand that homosexuality is not in any sense a kind of *conduct*.'[4] In contradiction, a contemporary Christian psychiatrist says: 'A homosexual is a man or woman who engages in homosexual acts. I have chosen my definition carefully.'[5] And another psychiatrist says: 'There are really no homosexuals; only individuals with homosexual orientations and problems.'[6] No doubt they are concerned over the fact that by imposing rigid classifications on people, as when we say 'he/she is homosexual', we not only determine attitudes but also hopes.

However, some people appear to have exclusive or extreme homosexual tendencies – '6' on the Kinsey scale (where '0' represents an exclusively heterosexual orientation). What do we say about such people? How many are there? What causes their condition?

How widespread?
The Working Party refers to the spread of homosexual practices, and refers to Kinsey's studies of homosexuals in the United States. It tells us that 'according to Kinsey, writing in terms of sexual *acts*, four per cent of white American males were exclusively homosexual throughout their lives after the onset of adolescence ...' (para 37 – italics mine). After detailing other statistics the conclusion is reached: 'While more than one in three men have been *actively* homosexual for a period of at least three years between the ages of sixteen and fifty-five, it must be stressed that only about one in twenty-four had been exclusively so, the remaining majority being ambisexual' (para 38 – italics mine). This needs to be

qualified, however. Kinsey was not 'writing in terms of sexual *acts*' nor did he and his colleagues conclude that 'one in three men had been *actively* homosexual' for the period specified. He said 'one male out of every three' had 'at least incidental homosexual experience or reactions'. When Kinsey worked out his scale and allotted people to it, no distinction was made between orientation and activity. Kinsey (*et al*) wrote: 'It will be observed that the rating which an individual receives has a dual basis. It takes into account his overt sexual experience and/or his psycho-sexual reactions ... In each classification there are persons who have had *no experience* or a minimum of overt sexual experience, but in the same classification there may also be persons who have had hundreds of sexual contacts' (italics mine).[7] This means that people high on the Kinsey scale can be there without having any homosexual activity what-soever!

Kinsey's statistics have been very influential in thinking on homosexuality with his 'one in twenty-four'. But in evaluating these figures, we need to remember two things. First, of the thousands of case studies (12,214 to be precise) on which the conclusions were based, fifty per cent appear to have been contacts developed through the many lectures given about the Kinsey programme of 1938–47, ie people who attended the lectures. 'Perhaps 50,000 persons have heard about the research through lectures, and perhaps half of the histories now in hand have come in consequence of such contacts.'[8] But in the early 1940's the type of person who would go to a lecture on sex research was probably atypical of the population. Even in today's permissive society, a lecture on explicitly sexual subjects might be self-selecting. How much more so in the 1940's.

Secondly, while lectures were best suited for middle-class contacts, 'practically all of the contacts at lower levels, and many of those at other levels, have depended upon introductions made by persons who had previously contributed their own histories. One who has not already given a history is not usually effective as a "contact man". Contact men and women have often spent considerable time and have gone to considerable pains to interest their friends and acquaintances.'[9] But here is another factor of selectivity. Those willing to give their sexual life stories were not 'random'. They were those who had been persuaded to do so by friends already involved. Presumably many did not want to reveal their personal sexual histories. We may presume that those who were more sexually experienced were more willing to speak. Kinsey admits that 'the restrained histories have on the whole been the more difficult to get'.[10] Also there is some suggestion that even the few groups which provided a hundred per cent samples were selected by their initial response to the project.[1]

Other people have done work on the incidence of homosexuality apart from Kinsey. Some of their studies have revealed that homosexual behaviour seems to vary from place to place and culture to culture. Anthropological studies have indicated this. According to Ford and Beach in nearly forty per cent of the societies for which information is available 'homosexual activities on the part of adults are reported to be totally absent, rare, or carried on only in secrecy'.[12] Statistics on sexual behaviour, of course, are notoriously difficult to come by. It would be a brave man or woman therefore who claimed to know the incidence of homosexuals in the United Kingdom. For the sake of the argument most people would use Kinsey's statistics. Writing, however, of homosexuals one British doctor has categorically stated: 'Their prevalence in the population at large is not known.'[13] The last (1973) BMA pamphlet on *Homosexuality* sums things up like this: 'Nobody really knows for sure. The most reliable statistics to date are American (!), but these were collected some years ago and do not necessarily apply to England.' It then guesses at one in twenty-five males. But that appears to be a simple echo of Kinsey. The proportion of homosexuals may be significantly smaller.

Cause

What is the cause of a homosexual condition? The Working Party gives the following account: 'The development of homosexuality does not seem to depend on any gross genetic, gonadal or phenotypic abnormality. Its origins seem much more likely to lie in hormonal imprinting in embryogenesis and/or in the rearing process by parents or parental surrogates' (para 81).

The 'and/or' draws attention to the fact that essentially there are two types of theory with regard to the causation of homosexuality – either (i) 'biological' or (ii) 'environmental – psychological'.

The 'biological' theories have included the view that homosexuality is a genetic aberration. This was current after Kallman's studies on twins (1952), but as the Working Party admits these studies have been criticised (para 57). As one authority on homosexuality sums it up: 'at this point in time it appears safe to agree with James (1970) that "there is now little support for the notion that homosexuality has a predominantly inherited basis".'[14]

Another 'biological' theory is to treat homosexuality as an endocrine disorder – ie homosexuality is 'hormonal'. The evidence for this has come mainly through work on animals (monkeys and rats). In the nature of the case the evidence is problematic. Medical ethics, properly, do not allow experimentation on human foetuses prior to birth. In any case, it is not yet clear whether the relationship between hormonal levels and behaviour is one of cause and effect or interaction. Generally it is felt that hormonal factors at most would only be a contributory factor to a homosexual condition.

More weight is now given to the second type of 'theory' – the 'environmental – psychological'. This type of theory concentrates on the childhood period as being significant in sexual development. Morally speaking, of course, the distinction as to whether a homosexual is made rather than born is a fine one. This is because moral responsibility will

63

hardly be affected by whether a person's condition was influenced prior to his or her birth or in the very early years. We would not want to 'blame' a person for his childhood. But the possibilities of change are probably felt to be more 'open' if social learning theories are given sufficient weight.

Parental influence has naturally received attention in these theories. A dominant mother and a passive father (or a host of other permutations) have been seen as contributory factors to a homosexual condition. Here, homosexuality is viewed from the perspective of the 'family constellation'; it is then sometimes felt helpful to see a person as being more afraid of the opposite sex than attracted to the same sex. This attraction is the result of fear, not a 'thing in itself'.

The importance of social reinforcement and 'modelling' in helping the child to a proper sex orientation have also been stressed.

As these theories have been developed they have led to a 'shift' away from the idea that the homosexual person is 'born, not made' to a concentration on the rearing process. Lawrence Hatterer, an American psychiatrist, in his book *Changing Homosexuality in the Male* argues that homosexuality is learned behaviour and that psychiatrists are coming to agree 'that homosexuals are not born but made, and that genetic, hereditary, constitutional, glandular or hormonal factors have no significance in causing homosexuality'.[15] Possibly. At least, that is one view.

But, of course, parental influence does not always account for the child's development. After all there are dominant mothers and passive fathers (and vice versa) who raise heterosexual children and more normal parents who raise homosexual children. Perhaps society at large is influential! And what about homosexual seduction as an important contributory factor? Para 42 states, without argument: 'Any propensity towards homosexual orientation does not seem to be increased in the case of boys affected by this practice.' But on this a clinical psychologist has written, in correspondence: 'the statement . . . deserves thorough documentation.

It is at least controversial and possibly untrue. I have certainly read opinions recently ... which confirm my clinical impression that a number of those presenting as homosexuals relate this to a significant seduction experience as boys. I have also seen papers suggesting that there is no link. Faced with a choice, I favour the positive evidence.'

Responsibility

So much for some of the things that are said about the cause of homosexuality. It cannot now be said that it is simply like 'left-handedness'. However, for the moment, let us assume that it is. Would this automatically mean that homosexuality was morally neutral in the same way as left-handedness is morally neutral? The Working Party assumes the answer is yes. They use the analogy of 'red hair' rather than 'left-handedness'. 'If homosexuality was, for instance, genetically determined in the same way as red hair, then taking a moral attitude towards it might seem irrelevant' (para 32). But would it necessarily be irrelevant? Supposing a given action is completely determined by a person's genetic endowment. This does not *ipso facto* nullify 'moral attitudes' towards it or mean that we cannot make moral judgements. There are certain instances where we clearly can make judgements or evaluations. If, for example, a person's genetic endowment led to 'child-battering' we would obviously want to say that responsibility was diminished, but at the same time we would evaluate the act as wrong and consider it something to be prevented.

Indeed Christian theology wants to say that there *is* responsibility within genetically determined conditions. All human beings are genetically determined to a certain extent. Yet we are all 'responsible' before God, and we are all predisposed to act in selfish and 'irresponsible' ways. The gospel, as we have said, is the offer of divine grace in Christ to forgive, heal and 'redeem' us in conditions of powerlessness and sin. Our chief responsibility is to receive that gift of grace in love and obedience. Then our 'genetic condition' can often provide the raw material which Christian obedience can redirect, if not renew. This is the case with those many homosexuals who see the celibate life as a positive opportunity for the service of both God and the world.

Treatment
Along with the 'shift' towards seeing homosexual responses as significantly influenced by 'social learning', there has grown a greater optimism with regard to treatment. If behaviour is 'learnt', there is perhaps a better chance of it being unlearnt.

But is there a possibility of change? How effective is treatment, medically speaking? There are indeed problems. There are practical problems in terms of the more psychoanalytical forms of treatment. 'The doctor sees the man at most once or twice a week ... basically the method is a question of two people talking ... the psychiatrist is no part of the man's world; he talks to him in a segregated and insulated setting at intervals of several days. Yet the doctor's job is to counteract the influences that work continuously and pervasively at the man's home, at his work and leisure, in fact throughout his waking hours.'[16] Then in some other forms of therapy there are certain, and sometimes serious, ethical questions that need to be raised.

However the facts are that in some cases success is being recorded. Bieber reported in 1962 some small success (twenty-seven per cent) with his psychoanalytical methods. In 1967 Feldman and MacCulloch reported fifty-eight per cent success with their adversive techniques. Thus John Court has written: 'It is now possible to refute categorically the view that the homosexual condition cannot be effectively treated.' He would indeed be the first to admit that 'the exclusively homosexual, the older person, and the one forced into treatment by external pressures are particularly unlikely to benefit from treatment'[17] – optimism tempered with realism.

Michael Schofield also reflects this realism when he said:

66

'Personalities are not often changed on the couch. They are much more likely to be changed through inter-action with other people than in the isolated setting of the psychiatric clinic.'[18] This surely is where the Church of Jesus Christ is so important. It should be able to provide a caring and supportive community. There must not be a false optimism. This is true for both the doctor and the pastor. The doctor has to be cautious before jumping on every new treatment bandwagon. Success while growing is still limited. So too must the pastor be careful. But today there is evidence of the transforming power of the Holy Spirit in relation to all kinds of human problems and conditions, including the homosexual condition.

Take a clergyman who tells us: 'Of the twenty-one homosexuals that I have counselled, ten have rejected the route I have outlined . . . as being too difficult. The eleven who have followed . . . have found release.'[19] In a BMA report given as long ago as 1955 to the Wolfenden Committee there was an appendix entitled *Conversion and the Homosexual*. It instanced case histories where the power of the Holy Spirit had changed lives. Elsewhere in this book we record more examples. The story of 'treatment' for the homosexual is not complete without this dimension.

In all forms of treatment the person has got to *want* to change. There has to be motivation and a desire for help. This seems universally agreed. How important, therefore, that the Church should not weaken these desires or motivations by weakening its stand over the heterosexual ideal as God's intention.

Illness, variant or deviant
The stance of the Working Party becomes especially clear when we come to para 77: 'Consideration of treatment requires us first to decide whether homosexuality is rightly understood as a pathological state, ie an illness. If it is not, but is, rather, a variant in sexual development (a view we hold), treatment would be appropriate only if the condition

was unacceptable to or unwanted by the individual concerned.'

The Working Party therefore has the 'view' that homosexuality is a 'variant' and not an 'illness'. But the Working Party should not simply have opposed either variant or illness; writing from a Christian viewpoint they have three categories to choose from. These are that homosexuality could be classed as (i) a variant in sexual development, or (ii) a pathological state, or (iii) a manifest part of fallen and disordered nature (a view that Christians have traditionally held). The practical implications of taking the view that homosexuality is only a variant are underlined in para 79. 'It should be stressed that it does not follow from the fact that some people can be helped to change in this way, that all could, let alone should, receive such help.' Although treatment is available, the Working Party is suggesting that it *should not* be available for some homosexuals! Of course, if this were a reference to not enforcing treatment, there would be no quarrel. But if it means that a doctor should not try, while respecting his patient's integrity, to steer an 'avowed and practising' homosexual into a heterosexual way of life, that is questionable. Some doctors would say impossible!

But there are no scientific or empirical grounds for deciding that homosexuality is only a variant. It depends on what one's concept of the 'normal' is. If you take the biblical or traditional Christian position, you will say that homosexuality is not a variant but a deviant.

The concept of the 'normal' can be defined in various ways. We can define it in terms of a situation where there is sufficient healthy functioning, or in terms of 'an ideal' or in terms of the statistical average. But for 'man' and what is normal for him, the Christian surely is committed to a 'norm' which is set by Jesus Christ and God's revelation. Christ after all reveals true manhood as well as deity.

It is interesting to note that there clearly is a problem faced by those who, along with the Working Party, say that homosexuality is a variant. In the USA in 1974 the American Psychiatric Association voted against calling homosexuality pathological or a disease. However, a recent poll of psychiatrists published in the journal *Medical Aspects of Homosexuality* noted that sixty-nine per cent of those approached still answered 'yes' to the question, 'is homosexuality usually a pathological adaptation?' with eighteen per cent answering 'no', and thirteen per cent uncertain.[20]

The possibility of a pathology is evidenced in the Working Party's report, where it admits: 'A neurotic depressive reaction is common in homosexual people' (para 75). It argues that 'this may be precipitated by conflict over being a homosexual person in contemporary society'. Who is to say? Studies in the past revealed a high rate of suicides among homosexuals.[21] Is this society's fault for being non-accepting of homosexuals, or, as is possible, is it due to psychological pressure inherent in the formation of homosexual relationships? In that case although the person would not be classed as pathological, the relationship would be.

Gender and orientation

We need to look at definitions again. But first we need to be reminded that in the current discussion of homosexuality biologically abnormal sexual conditions, as in the case of hermaphrodites, are treated as quite distinct problems.

We then find we can distinguish between (i) sexual differentiation, (ii) sexual identity, (iii) sexual role and (iv) sexual preference.

Sexual (or gender) differentiation (i) is the 'given' – the physical distinction in the (human) species between male and female. Sexual identity (ii) (subjectively speaking) comes when we perceive ourselves to be either male or female. Sexual role (iii) refers to how we act out our sexual or gender identity. This, of course, varies considerably from culture to culture and family to family. Sexual preference (iv) is to do with the choice of the object of our sexual desires and drives. This is 'normally' and 'should be' a desire for the opposite sex.

The exercise of human 'choice' varies with regard to differentiation, identity, role and preference. There is no choice as to sexual differentiation (i). That is physically 'given', and genetically determined. Sexual identity (ii) what we perceive ourselves to be, whether male or female, is learned. There is little choice for us. It is learned both from the 'given' (our external genitalia) *and* from society's expectations of us. But here *society* can exercise choice. There is also choice, this time our own, in sexual role (iii) and sexual preference (iv). The choice may be hard and sometimes difficult, and the fault in wrong choices may not lie with the individuals concerned (nor necessarily with their parents – there is a 'sin of the world'). But how a man or woman acts out sexual roles and sexual preferences is up to him or her. They are responsible; but the total responsibility is not only individual but corporate as well. The wider community determines both what is acceptable and what is expected.

It is because there is a corporate dimension to this that society's views and values on what is appropriate sexually are important. One of the reasons why Christians are worried about the confusion over homosexuality and one of the reasons why the Working Party's Report is being criticised is because to make homosexuality a neutral sexual variant is to mute the call of God with respect to sexual role and sexual preference. This, as we shall see, is made clear in the Bible. If society, aided by some within the Church, is confused as to sexual role and confused as to proper sexual preference, not only is there disorder with regard to God's order, but an unfair strain put upon those persons who are trying to learn their sexual roles and their sexual preferences, particularly the young. This learning process in part is influenced by society's expectations.

Conclusion

'At present medical science can give only a very incomplete account of the formation of sexual orientation. *What we do know suggests that people have the responsibility for de-*

ciding whether or not to express their orientation in sexual acts' (para 86 – italics mine). With that we all agree.

NOTES

1 *Towards a Quaker View of Sex*, revised edition (London: Friends House Service Committee, 1964) p 26
2 *Hansard*: Sexual Offences (Amendment) Bill (18) 14 June 1977
3 *Report of the Committee on Homosexual Offences and Prostitution* (HMSO: 1957) p 16, 35
4 *The Problem of Homosexuality* (CIB: 1954) p 7
5 John White, op cit p 105
6 Roger Moss, op cit p 42
7 A. C. Kinsey (*et al*), *Sexual Behaviour in the Human Male* (W. B. Saunders, Eastbourne: 1948) pp 650 and 647
8 Ibid p 38
9 Ibid pp 38–39
10 Ibid p 103
11 Ibid p 95
12 G. S. Ford and E. A. Beach, *Patterns of Sexual Behaviour* (London: 1965) p 136
13 G. C. Scorer, *The Bible and Sex Ethics today* (London: 1966) p 119
14 J. H. Court, *Homosexuality – a scientific and Christian Perspective*, in Interchange, 1973, 30, pp 24–40; quoting B. James, 'Homosexuality', in C. G. Costello (ed), *Symptoms of Psychopathology* (Wiley, Chichester: 1970)
15 Lawrence Hatterer, *Changing Homosexuality in the Male* (New York: 1970) p 47 in Don Williams, op cit p 27
16 Michael Schofield, op cit p 167
17 J. H. Court, op cit
18 Michael Schofield, op cit p 168
19 *Healing for the Homosexual* (Oklahoma City: 1978) p 49
20 Richard Lovelace, *Homosexuality and the Church* (Lamp, London: 1978) p 114
21 Michael Schofield, op cit p 189

4 BIBLICAL ISSUES

Perhaps one of the most significant features of chapter three of the Report, entitled 'Homosexuality: the Biblical Evidence', is that while the Working Party has said that it wants to view homosexuality within the context of sexuality as a whole, its actual concentration is firmly on passages in the Bible which deal explicitly with homosexuality. It may have been more helpful to have focused on and started with biblical material that deals with the broader issues of sex.

If one is wanting to have an overview of sexuality, the place surely to begin is Genesis 1–3, where we have material crucial to any theology of sexuality, and material, incidentally, which is affirmed by Jesus himself. However, the Report's treatment of homosexual behaviour begins with 'actual homosexual behaviour' (para 88) and the Sodom Episode (para 89).

It may at this point be worth noting that the Board for Social Responsibility itself, although reflecting differences of approach among its members to the biblical text, reported that 'the treatment in this chapter of the biblical material read to most members of the Board, including some who support its conclusions, as an "explaining away" of the evidence; it was seen as minimising the fact, noted by the Working Party themselves, that "what evidence there is seems clearly to show condemnation of homosexual behaviour" (para 106). An interpretation is often put upon the biblical text which gives the impression that the conclusion came first and influenced the way in which the evidence was interpreted' (para A4). Examples were then given. We can follow these up.

The Sodom story
First let us take the Sodom story (paras 89–96). This comes
from Genesis 19 and has already been referred to earlier in
this book.

Three sins are recorded in the narrative – the denial of
guest rights, rape and homosexual behaviour. No wonder
Sodom in the biblical tradition epitomises general corruption. Homosexual activity was only one fault of its sinfulness. But it was a fault. So as later Judaism came into
touch with homosexuality in the Hellenistic world of the last
Testament Sodom was often remembered for its homosexual aspect of Sodom's sinfulness. By the time of the New
centuries BC, it was natural (and right) to recall the homosexual sin.

As we have already seen, the Working Party reflects some
shifting in the thinking about homosexuality. It reflects a
'shift' here. Sherwin Bailey, who was formerly the central
lecturer for the Church of England's Moral Welfare Council
published a very influential book entitled *Homosexuality
and the Western Christian Tradition*. In it he argued that
the Christian tradition has misunderstood the Sodom story,
for it is not really about homosexuality but only about inhospitality. However, as Michael Green has earlier pointed
out in this book the verb 'know' in the account does refer to
'homosexual intercourse'.

'Bailey may perhaps have overstated his case,' is how
John McNeill, a radical Roman Catholic, puts it.[1] But
Bailey's thesis has been very influential. It 'undercut the
popular notion that toleration of homosexual behaviour is a
sign of national decay'.[2] In his book he argued that this is
why the state as well as the Church has been opposed to
homosexuality. The Working Party is now admitting that
Bailey may have been wrong: 'It seems likely, therefore, that
the Sodom story does contain a reference to homosexual
behaviour' (para 90).

So in the Old Testament and in the New Testament when

73

there are references to Sodom, a 'package' of sins would often have been in mind.

But someone will still ask, 'Is it not rape alone that is being condemned in the Sodom story? Perhaps the Bible is not bothered with whether it was homosexual or heterosexual? Can we be sure that the narrative is positively against homosexual behaviour as such?' The answer is 'yes', if we see it in the total context of those early chapters of Genesis, which include Genesis 1–3. For these three chapters not only provide the foundation for biblical sexual ethics, but supply the interpretive background for the chapters that follow, including chapter nineteen, the story of Sodom.

Genesis 1–3
In Genesis 1 we have foundational theology. Genesis 1:27 is the first and one of the most important verses on sexuality: 'So God created *man* in his own image, in the image of God he created *him*; male and female he created *them*.' This is the fundamental assertion that 'man', the human, is properly understood when seen as 'male and female' together. 'Man'/'him' is here equated with 'male and female'/'them'. 'The primal form of humanity is thus the fellowship of man and woman.'[3] It is not man and man, or woman and woman, but man and woman. This is, therefore, the lie to the old unisex mythologies. It is a clear statement that 'to be human is to share humanity with the opposite sex'.[4]

The narrative makes it clear that 'man' is the pinnacle of God's creation and is the enjoyer of God's special mandate to be fruitful, to multiply and to 'have dominion'. 'And God blessed them, and God said to them, "Be fruitful and multiply." ' (v 28). However, the primary purpose in being created a pair is not that the male and the female should be able to fulfil more efficiently that mandate, but rather that they should be creators of fellowship, companionship, and community. The command to procreate (v 28) is separated from the description of their existence as male and female

74

(v 27). This appears to be underlined in Genesis 2, where the affirmation is that 'it is not good that the man should be alone' (v 18). The solution, however, to that problem of isolation or loneliness is not the creation of another man; rather it is the creation of woman. It is not a man who will fulfil man's desire for community, but someone who is distinctly 'other'.

But this is not the last word that can be found in these early chapters of the Bible on sexuality. We have to take note of Genesis 3, where man learns the hard way that the fulfilled life is only achieved through living according to the limits set and permissions given by God. For the temptation comes to the pair to live beyond these permissions and to act according to their own will. The result is tragic. On the one hand there is a separation of the man from the woman – symbolised by the covering of their nakedness. On the other hand, there is a separation of both from God himself – symbolised by their going into hiding. The result of this disobedience (commonly, of course, called 'the Fall') is that the sexual roles of the pair are confused and disordered. Genesis 3:16 shows that there is now servility and domination instead of full companionship.

Thus 'the Fall' can be said to produce sexual role disorder. It does not necessarily produce sexual identity disorder. The woman still perceives herself to be a woman, and the man perceives himself to be a man, for they were conscious of their 'nakedness'. They still retain their 'given' sexuality or gender differentiation as God had created them, ie as male and female. However, the way they live out their sexual roles is suspect. It is not as God intended. Instead of mutuality there is subservience. We can see these chapters as indicating sexual disorder as being due to the Fall.

But this is not something that the Report discusses. Yet it is of course of the essence of the question. Para 121 ends with the question referring to homosexuals: 'Is their condition an aspect of the fallenness of creation, or is there a place for them in the divine order wherein they may fulfil the sexuality which is theirs?' We are then promised that the following chapter will deal with this 'central question'. But no analysis or answer is given.

Traditionally the Genesis narrative has been taken to argue that God has given us the gift of being male *or* female, while at the same time he utters a call to us to live heterosexually – males *with* females, and this in monogamous marriage. That call may be rejected. But that does not deny the validity of the call. Of course it is an open question how far the rejection of any call (or demand) of God is thoroughly 'free', without any predisposing factors. (This is relevant if people are at all 'conditioned' in their homosexual orientation.) Certainly there was 'pressure' on Eve in the form of the serpent. But the narrative appears to be less interested in the mechanics of human response; it is interested rather in the responsibility that man has. Clearly he (or she) is *sufficiently free* to obey or disobey. He (or she) *ought* to obey.

But what about the 'created order' as such? Can we talk about a 'creation ideal'? The Working Party seems to be suggesting 'No'. After giving us a fair analysis of the created order with reference to Genesis 1 (para 99) it seems to be suggesting (para 119) that because the Church abolished the distinction between clean and unclean animals, *anything* within the created order can be called into question. This, of course, does not do justice to the fact that Jesus seems to have endorsed the sexual teaching of Genesis 1–3 when he referred to its teaching on marriage (Mark 10:7–9). At the same time he and the apostles set light to the distinctions between what was clean and what was unclean (Matthew 15:11).

Leviticus

In Leviticus there are prohibitions on homosexual activity. 'You shall not lie with a male as with a woman; it is an abomination' (18:22); and 'If a man lies with a male as with a woman, both of them have committed an abomination'

76

(20:13). It is said that such behaviour characterised Israel's Canaanitish neighbours (eg 20:23). So the Report argues that Leviticus prohibits homosexual acts really for being a species of idolatry: 'This, of course, is not to deny that homosexual practices as such are condemned in Leviticus but only to underline that they are seen as peculiarly characteristic of heathen religion and society and that in Leviticus this is *the basic reason* for avoiding them' (para 100 – italics mine). The implication here is that homosexuality is wrong fundamentally not because it is a violation of God's created order, but because it is a way of expressing identity with pagan Canaanitish cults. Or put another way, it was not so much that homosexuality was wrong in itself as that at the time it had specific religious overtones, and it was these religious overtones that were being opposed. The conclusion is then left to be drawn that when these overtones no longer ring out, homosexual behaviour may become permissible!

But how true is it that homosexuality was *particularly* a feature of Canaanitish religion? It is sometimes said that the 'male cult-prostitutes' referred to from time to time in the Old Testament (para 88) indicate cultic homosexuality. But as the Working Party argues, 'given the fact that such cultic prostitution was concerned with the promotion of fertility', such male prostitutes were probably for services to women, not men. Homosexuality when it was common, would thus have been a feature of pagan *social life in general* rather than specifically 'religious' life.

There is no evidence that homosexuality was 'religious' (in the cultic sense) among Israel's neighbours. In theory Israel's neighbours were also against homosexual practices: 'The Egyptians numbered corruption of boys among the sins which the soul repudiated at its judgement, the Assyrians penalised homosexual acts by statute, and both regarded passive sodomy in particular as derogatory to human dignity – a humiliation meet for defeated enemies or convicted paederasts.'[5]

The existence of homosexuality among Israel's neighbours

in the Old Testament is, therefore, likely to have been seen not so much as a mark of idolatry as a mark of the social degeneracy that idolatry led to. It was not part and parcel of idolatrous worship. Rather the pagan cults, with their stress on fertility rites, would have created a moral climate in which homosexual practice would thrive.

It is no doubt right to see in these chapters of Leviticus the Old Testament concern for 'the preservation of the family group' (para 110) as bound up with the prohibition on homosexual practice. But to imply that the Old Testament 'family group' is a cultural phenomenon and so therefore the rules relating to it were without universal application is very doubtful (para 97). No doubt aspects of the Old Testament family life pattern are irrelevant for today. But if the development of Old Testament notions on the family is based on Genesis 1-3, we cannot treat all these insights in so cavalier a fashion.

What is inescapable from a survey of the Old Testament material is that homosexual practice is clearly condemned. It was remembered as being part of the lifestyle of Israel's ancient neighbours. When God's people met up with homosexual excesses subsequently in their history they realised that God had called them to a different way, as the Law reminded them. This was his 'created way' and therefore the way to true fulfilment.

The Old Testament, therefore, gives us a moral insight which is opposed to current 'cultural fashions'. And more specifically in the prohibition on homosexual actions you have a call to God's people to be different and refrain from what everyone else is doing! One of the moral themes constant to the Old Testament and to the New Testament is that the people of God are *not* to conform to the sexual immoralities of the world around them. God has shown them and called them to a better way. It is admitted in para 106 that 'many' may hold this view.

Before we leave these verses of Leviticus, we need to see them as part of the 'whole'. The verses on homosexuality in chapters eighteen and twenty come from what is normally described as the 'Holiness Code' (Leviticus 17:1–26:46). In this section of Leviticus God is seen to be the transcendant holy God and the result is a deepening moral sense as the holiness of God is revealed. This leads to an awareness that in the relationship between the sexes not everything 'goes' for the people of God. It needs to be remembered that the penalties for unchastity and sexual disorder are here more severe than those imposed in Babylonia. Such penalties thus underline the 'seriousness' of the sexual dimension.

These chapters are in fact indications within the format of a legal code that personal morality for the people of God is not a matter of indifference or pure private choice. There is no 'spiritual gnosis' here. Rather it is a rugged assertion that social and personal development and godly obedience must go hand-in-hand.

To repeat, these chapters are stressing that the visible community of the people of God is to be distinct from those outside that community. If that is not relevant for the Church of Jesus Christ today, what is? This is the thesis of so much of the New Testament, not in a world-denying way, but in a truly world-affirming way. The central teaching of the New Testament (and in effect of the Old) is that the world is in need of redemption, and the Church is to be a sign pointing towards that redemption in Jesus Christ, by being a light in the midst of darkness!

The New Testament
The Report goes on to imply an 'argument from silence' – the relative silence in the Bible about homosexuality. It adds also the argument that we now have superior knowledge. 'There is comparatively little about homosexuality' (para 106) in the Bible. To that it must be replied, in the words of Professor G. R. Dunstan, 'First, that what little there is is without exception condemnatory, and secondly that we err if we expect the Bible to match in proportion the obsessions of a modern generation.'

79

There are inevitably certain omissions in this section of the Report on the biblical material. It is unfair to expect a complete survey. But one omission needs specially to be noted. It is the words of Jesus which relate directly to homosexuality. They have been mentioned earlier in this book, but they are not commented on in the Report. Matthew 19:12: 'There are eunuchs who have been so from birth, and there are eunuchs who have been made eunuchs by men, and there are eunuchs who have made themselves eunuchs for the sake of the kingdom of heaven.' Jesus, as seen from the context, here seems to be teaching that some people do not experience heterosexual marriage because of choice, while others because of the fallenness of the world – either the fallenness of men (castration), or the fallenness of nature (birth).

Jesus in the New Testament presupposes heterosexuality at every point and genital sex for marriage alone. The alternative, as we can see from this passage, is abstinence. Jesus, of course, himself argues that the sins of Sodom and Gomorrah are indeed no worse than the sins of people who disregarded his claims and yet who probably outwardly were respectable from a conventional point of view. In the scale of values, the decadence of Sodom is by no means the worst of sins. 'Jesus dealt with the sensual sinners incomparably more leniently than he did with the sinners who committed the sins of the spirit and cupidity.'[6] In terms of the biblical teaching on how the Christian should view and relate to homosexual activity, this is important. For this suggests a judgement on all the misguided and cruel homophobia that does exist in certain Christian circles. At the same time hypocrisy of various sorts may be tolerated in those very same circles. However, Jesus *does* identify Sodom and Gomorrah with sin; they are seen to be symbols of godless materialism (Luke 17:28–30). He also seems to imply the wicked inhospitality of Sodom in Luke 10:12.

The Report also does not refer to the statement on homosexuality in Jude 7 and 8: 'Just as Sodom and Gomorrah, and the surrounding cities, which likewise acted immorally and indulged in unnatural lust, serve as an example by undergoing a punishment of eternal fire. Yet in like manner these men in their dreamings defile the flesh.' The importance of this is that here is canonical witness that *in the Church* there can be those persons who in fact 'pervert the grace of God into licentiousness' (v 4). There appear to have been practising homosexuals in the Church. There were those who 'defiled the flesh' (v 8). However obscure all this may be, Jude indicates a clear 'no' to homosexual practices within the Church of Jesus Christ.

The Report also has no discussion of Romans 7 and the biblical analysis of 'the weakness of the will'. It has no mention of the biblical material on forgiveness, or on the power of the Holy Spirit. There is nothing on 'the Cross' or the experience of suffering, and how that can be redemptive.

St Paul
However, the Report does discuss St Paul. About him (and other New Testament writers) the Report has this to say: 'The real nub of the discussion, however, is whether the authors of the New Testament epistles had in view the homosexual *condition* or merely certain homosexual *practices*' (para 105). It is then claimed in para 112 that the recognition of a homosexual bias or 'personality' is comparatively recent and 'largely unknown to the biblical writers'. The question follows 'How far is it proper to apply the biblical prohibition of homosexuality to these people whom they could not possibly have had in view?'

But this surely is an improper argument from silence. In any case the New Testament writers were probably not ignorant of this distinction. We have just seen how Jesus distinguishes 'eunuchs from birth' (p 80). Paul certainly did not have the vocabulary of 'condition' and 'practice' (in any case the Bible is not a handbook of sexual psychology). But he was capable of distinguishing between 'conditions' and 'practices' in other areas of behaviour. Someone who was

81

aware that the 'flesh' and 'the spirit' were in conflict *within* the Christian person, was clearly aware that disordered dispositions of various sorts were latent (a condition) in everyone. His worry with his friends in the New Testament churches (for example in Corinth) was that some of these were surfacing and being 'practised' in the Christian community.

With this evidence, we can ask whether Paul would have condemned a person with what today would be classified as 'a homosexual orientation' but who forewent homosexual activity. The answer surely is 'no', he would not. Paul indeed accepted former practising homosexuals in Corinth (1 Corinthians 6:11). What he unambiguously condemned was the practice of homosexuality. This is nowhere clearer than in Romans 1:26–27. 'For this reason God gave them up to dishonourable passions. Their women exchanged natural relations for unnatural, and the men likewise gave up natural relations with women and were consumed with passion for one another, men committing shameless acts with men and receiving in their own persons the due penalty for their error.'

Paul, we note, was not afraid to take issue with people. He does so in Romans 1 and 2. In Romans 1 he begins from a theology of nature and argues that homosexual behaviour is the result of God's judgement on sin. His main subject is not homosexuality but the rejection of God. The consequences (homosexual behaviour) serve to highlight this rejection.

Paul argues that God's judgement (his 'wrath' v 8) is sometimes to be seen in terms of self-induced suffering. Men and women reject him; he respects their freedom, and allows them to do what they like (in this instance in terms of sexual or homosexual preferences) *with the inevitable consequences*, 'receiving in their own persons the due penalty for their error' (v 27).

From this we note two things. First, that Paul is more concerned with the *original* cause (selfish independence from God), rather than the result of that (homosexual behaviour); the latter is a *symptom*. Paul is not homophobic! Nevertheless he sees homosexual activity as wrong.

Secondly, it is clear that Paul is talking about homosexual activity which relates to a tragic homosexual lifestyle (v 27). It thus appears that Paul is talking here, not about a temporary, careless lapse into same-sex activity (what is called 'perversion') as some people have argued; his language (certainly in terms of the results of sin) is more appropriate to those who have a homosexual condition.

The final degradation for Paul seems, however, not to be in the case of those with a tragic homosexual lifestyle, but in the case of those who 'though they know God's decree that those who do such things deserve to die, they not only do them, but approve those who practise them (v 32). This would be a description, not of those who merely engage in homosexual practices; but of those who are *avowed* and *practising* homosexuals. An 'avowed' homosexual is someone who wants to affirm his or her homosexuality as positive, good and to be celebrated. Such is the intention of the 'gay' movement of today!

But Paul's reason for identifying homosexuality as he has done is not to bring despair, gloom or a sense of fatalistic hopelessness. No, this is not his last word on the subject, but his first word. For Paul proceeds in chapter two to discuss, not the 'decadent pagan' who has rejected God, with one manifestation of this being homosexuality, but the 'respectable religious' person who rejoices in and assents to all that Paul has been saying. If the modern counterpart of chapter one is to be found in the homophile or gay organisations, the modern counterpart of the type of person Paul has in mind in chapter two will be found amongst those who support the Nationwide Festival of Light and amongst those, who like myself, are highly critical of the Working Party's Report. They must avoid the hypocritical sins he speaks of. The gist of chapter two is that those who judge pagan morality are equally guilty before God, if only they realised it. They too reject God if the truth were known, but this has quieter results. In his mercy, God has prevented all the *consequences* of that rejection from being worked out in their social and sexual experience. Their actual life programmes may therefore be happier. They may experience 'the joys of family life'. But in real terms, beneath all the veneer of anti-permissiveness and even biblicism or traditional catholic theology there can be a lovelessness and unrepenting hypocrisy, with regard to which Paul's words in chapter 2:5 are relevant: 'by your hard and impenitent heart you are storing up wrath for yourself on the day of wrath when God's righteous judgement will be revealed.'

Paul's concern, as was Jesus' concern with sexual sinners, was not to mark out practising homosexuals as worse than others. His concern was to show that practising homosexuals and respectable moralisers, in terms of God's standards, *all* fall short. This is the message of chapter three. 'There is no distinction . . . all have sinned and fall short of the glory of God' (v 23).

But the gospel, the reason why Paul is writing, is that this is not the last word. Indeed, to any social commentator of his generation, like Juvenal or Tacitus, Paul's remarks on homosexuality would have been self-evident and hardly needing to be said. He was not writing to shock a sensitive world, but simply to outline an argument. Paul's only reason for discussing in some detail practising homosexuals, and those who criticised them, is to show the relevance of the gospel of Christ for all.

It is for this reason that today an adequate treatment of the biblical understanding of homosexuality must include the biblical specifics of forgiveness and new life through the indwelling Holy Spirit. Nor do we have to suppose that Paul held to a myth of total victorious Christian living! It is more than likely that some of his Corinthian friends, for example, experienced the 'mystery of suffering' as they struggled at times to resist the Corinthian 'gay scene'. The context of 1 Corinthians 6 suggest that some did not resist these temptations, and so there was a danger of sexual disorder *within* the church. But at the end of the day, Paul can say: 'You were washed, you were sanctified, you were justified in the name of the Lord Jesus Christ and in the Spirit of our God' (v 11).

Cultural conditioning

Para 14 ends with the statement: 'There is nothing, it would seem in the New Testament to justify the Church in relaxing the condemnations of all homosexual behaviour which it inherits from the old covenant.' It then immediately goes on in para 115 to say: 'But the matter cannot simply be left there.' The reasons given are inadequate and unconvincing. First, Paul, we are told, was a child of his age and was as limited by its outlook as were the men of the Old Testament' – an extraordinary statement about the apostle of theological revolution from Judaism, the apostle who defied when necessary not only the Jewish and Roman authorities, but even his own Church leaders!

More needs to be said. When we look closely at the New Testament Church which Paul inhabited and the ethos of those early years, we find radical changes in attitudes towards human sexuality alongside a vigorous defence of God's creation plan. The attitude of both Jesus and Paul were different to those of many within Judaism. The man who indicated that homosexual practices were wrong, could fly in the face of convention and argue *against* the inferiority of woman. In Christ, Paul says, 'there is neither male nor female', rather we are all on a level, all 'sons of God, through faith' (Galatians 3:26 and 28).

One of the most interesting of these developments or about turns in attitudes towards human sexuality is seen in the account of Philip and the Ethiopian eunuch in Acts 8:26–39. Under the Old Testament law eunuchs were excluded from the community of the people of God: 'he whose testicles are crushed or whose male member is cut off shall not enter the assembly of the Lord' (Deuteronomy 23:1). But in the new Israel of the Messianic age (cf Isaiah 56:3–5) the eunuch was to have a place. The baptism of the Ethiopian eunuch showed that although in the past eunuchs may have been excluded, now they were to be welcomed into the Church.

So Paul, along with his fellow workers in the New Testament Church, was not 'a child of his age and . . . limited by its outlook'. The New Testament leadership decided to welcome eunuchs *in contrast to* the Old Testament ruling, but to forbid homosexual practices *following* the Old Testament ruling. They could make distinctions.

For these reasons we must disagree with the Working Party which in general seems to be suggesting that the biblical prohibitions against homosexual behaviour should be taken as relevant for Bible times, but not necessarily for today. That is what is meant by being 'culturally conditioned'. The biblical writers had not the advantages of modern science (para 112) otherwise they would have thought and spoken differently. But on the Working Party's own admission modern scientific evidence is inconclusive! How then or by what criterion can we judge the biblical evidence to be 'culturally conditioned'. To argue that because in the Old Testament the 'Holy War' principle (para 109) was seen as provisional and in need of reinterpreting and was therefore 'culturally conditioned', of itself is totally irrelevant to the question as to whether the principles regarding homosexual behaviour were and are provisional. Arguments need to be produced. Not everything was relative for the early Church. The Holy War was; but the Genesis teaching on marriage was *not*.

Conclusion

When we look at the Bible positively with regard to its teaching on sexuality, two things stand out. First, that it wholeheartedly celebrates sex as a gift of God. But in its genital expression it is reserved for heterosexual marriage; there it is to be enjoyed and desired, as evidenced by Proverbs 5:15–23 and the Song of Solomon.

Secondly, the Bible rejects without embarrassment and going into necessary detail all deviant and sinful sexual expression, of which homosexual genital activity is an example.

NOTES

1 John J. McNeill SJ, *The Church and the Homosexual* (London: 1977) p 47
2 Richard F. Lovelace, op cit, p 30
3 Don Williams, op cit, p 53
4 Ibid p 53
5 D. S. Bailey, *Homosexuality and the Western Christian Tradition* (London: 1955) p 36
6 Helmut Thielicke, *The Ethics of Sex* (J. Clark, Cambridge: 1964) p 278–79

5 'JUSTIFIABLY CHOOSE'

It has been particularly important to discuss the Working Party's treatment of Scripture. This is not only because of an unease about some of its methods of exegesis, but also because its conclusions on Scripture are accepted as premises for the development of the argument in its crucial chapter five – 'Theological and Ethical Considerations'. For here, having explained away, wrongly in our judgement, the Old Testament and Paul, the Working Party not unnaturally says, 'we do not think it would be possible on the strength of these passages alone to rule out of court the contentions of those … which would require us to revise the traditional judgement of the Church upon homosexuality' (para 126).

The Working Party then develops an argument which leads it to propose *revising the traditional historic teaching of the Church and permit genital homosexual relationships in certain circumstances.* They suggest that this is a middle way between 'totally forbidding' and 'explicitly sanctioning'; but if the Working Party can persuade itself, it will persuade few others who recognise that this is not a 'middle way' but a 'great divide'. It is something totally innovative in terms of Christian ethics. The divide is between admitting homosexual behaviour, even tentatively, and not admitting it at all. What are the arguments?

New thinking
The now much publicised conclusion that 'there are circumstances in which individuals may justifiably choose to enter into a homosexual relationship' (para 168) follows from the hinge argument in para 164: 'Traditionally the Church has ruled out homosexual practices entirely and we are not per-

suaded that this was a judgement that can now be seen to be totally erroneous or of merely temporary validity, for it does follow in principle from an understanding of sexuality which we believe to be fundamentally sound and defensible. But there is one important respect in which the situation has changed. It was assumed until quite recently that every mature individual was capable of a heterosexual response. It is now clear that for a significant proportion of the population this is not the case.'

This is a repeat of an earlier mis-statement (para 112) and is not true. It was not assumed until recently that all were capable of heterosexual relationships. As the Board for Social Responsibility has said, 'Any student of the canon law of marriage and of its interpretation in consistory courts of the medieval Church will recognise that this statement is false: the tests for impotence were ... explicit. Moreover, Jesus spoke of "eunuchs" who were so from their birth, and Clement of Alexandria writing in the third century, recorded a current interpretation of this to the effect that "some men, from their birth, have a natural sense of repulsion from a woman; and those who are naturally so constituted do well not to marry"' (para A7). The Working Party is not therefore justified in arguing that in this respect 'the situation has changed', that 'our new knowledge gives us a pastoral obligation not recognised before' and hence allows us to sanction some homosexual acts.

No choice

The Working Party says that it is concerned with 'those who have no choice in their homosexual orientation' (para 167). 'Indeed, it was the fact that they had no choice which weighed so heavily with us in our judgement that in certain circumstances a genital relationship might for such persons be justifiable' (para 262).

What do we mean by 'no choice'? We need to realise that 'no choice' in the present does not necessarily imply 'no choice' in the past. The Wolfenden Committee was concerned to point this out.[1] Take a man who is an alcoholic. There may have been some choices that he made in the past which have led him to a present situation in which he has no choice left. It may be similar with some homosexuals. Early choices may lead to a consolidated homosexual condition. One psychiatrist speaking of sexual activity in a homosexual relationship says, 'Each repetition of it may compound the need for more.'[2] This is in line with the Scriptural idea that whoever commits sin is the 'slave' of sin. Freedom goes.

Let us assume, however, that in some cases there have never been choices in regard to a person's homosexual orientation. Let us assume that it is proved to be totally inherited. What do we say then? It makes no difference. All have to understand that homosexual acts are sinful and so not permitted. We would say that such an orientation while disordered was not blameworthy. It was a disability. And as with many disabilities, freedom has to be curtailed. This is true of blindness, epilepsy, schizophrenia and other pathological conditions. But it is also true of non-pathological disabilities – the failure to pass a driving test, the inability to qualify for athletic competitions and so on. But as the earlier Church of England group reporting on homosexuality reminded us, 'some kind of limitation upon freedom to act as one desires is a necessary tension within all successful living'. Personal growth depends on 'what kind of attitude is adopted to the restricting factors'.[3]

If I can see such limitation as part of God's will, I can live with it, transcend it and use it creatively. If I believe it is an unnecessary imposition, I will get frustrated, self-pitying and bitter.

But it would be wrong to see God's limitations as there to frustrate us. They are there to help us reach our truest potential in the light of the realities of the fallen world, and also in the light of Christ and his glory. These limitations help us to become more like him, more useful to others, and, actually, more fulfilled ourselves.

It is hard to see how the 'no choice' argument can lead to

an overturning of the biblical prohibitions on homosexual practice.

The Working Party of course, nowhere is suggesting that people *must* express themselves homosexually. Indeed they argue that 'people have the responsibility for deciding whether *or not* to express their orientation in sexual acts' (para 86 – italics mine).

The Bible is irrelevant

If you do not want to be convinced by the biblical material it is easy enough to evade it. We can always ask for more evidence while never being open to conviction.

Shakespeare in *The Merchant of Venice* said, 'The Devil can cite Scripture for his purpose.' Scripture can be abused as well as used properly. But it also can be used, without abuse, but from different starting points or presuppositions. What are the Christian presuppositions? The general teaching of Jesus and his apostles. Being a Christian disciple means we believe that Jesus Christ and his apostles have something to teach us. So when we go to the Bible we go, in the words of that great Churchman of two centuries ago, Charles Simeon of Cambridge, 'content to sit as a learner at the feet of the holy Apostles, and (with) no ambition to teach them how they ought to have spoken'.[4]

That is an attitude, rather than a method of interpretation. It admits problems. We then have to use our minds. For instance, we may well admit that the Sodom story may have over-affected the attitude of the Church and state regarding homosexuality. Harsh laws appear to have been formulated against homosexuality because it was feared that the presence of homosexuality in the community would necessarily lead to a fate similar to Sodom's – actual destruction by brimstone and fire. 'As we survey the development of this (Christian) tradition,' wrote Sherwin Bailey, 'it becomes evident that the effect of the reinterpreted Sodom story upon the mind of the Church was in fact more profound than that of either the Levitical laws or the teaching of the New Testament.'[5]

91

But the teaching of the New Testament remains, even if the Sodom story has been over-interpreted. Nor is it good enough to say, as we have shown earlier, that the teaching of the New Testament can be changed everywhere because it is culturally conditioned. It is not culturally conditioned at every point. Its response to slavery may be culturally conditioned, for example. But its view of homosexuality is not like its view of slavery, where the seeds of slavery's undermining are already in the New Testament (the book of Philemon); furthermore slavery in the New Testament is in the wider biblical context of the release of slaves at the Jubilee in the Old Testament. No. Homosexual acts are condemned in both the Old *and* New Testaments.

Listen to the words of Professor Lovelace: 'The Scripture nowhere commends homosexual behaviour and condemns it in every place where it is mentioned. If we can interpret Scripture to endorse homosexual acts among Christians, we can make it endorse anything else we want to do or believe and our faith and practice are cut loose in a borderless chaos.'[6]

Natural Law

We are told by the Working Party that 'the traditional arguments for [homosexual acts being sinful] have tended to fall into two groups. There are those based upon Scriptural passages from both Old and New Testaments and those based upon Natural Law. Here indeed is one example of the diversity of Christian tradition, for the direct appeal to Scripture has been characteristically protestant and the appeal to nature characteristically catholic' (para 125).

Some might remark that this is significant in itself. For both protestant and catholic traditions converge at this point, over their condemnation of homosexual acts as being sinful.

Be that as it may, the Working Party criticises the Natural Law position – the appeal to nature – after giving an outline of the basic argument: 'The argument in its simplest form

92

holds that the sexual act by its very function is aimed at the transmission of life and that it is against nature, and consequently wrong, to engage in sexual activity in which this aim is frustrated. It concludes that each act of intercourse should be open to conception, and it is this conclusion that rules out contraception' (para 129). It also, obviously, rules out homosexual relationships and it is this version of the Natural Law argument that we often associate with the Roman Catholic Church.

As presented this is a veritable Aunt Sally. We need to remember that although the Roman Catholic Church is still officially against contraception, it is beginning to see 'the whole context in which human sexuality finds its meaning' (para 129) as it uses the approach from Nature. The Working Party recognises this. It is, therefore, unfair to dismiss the Natural Law argument because it can be justly criticised in its unrefined form. This, as we can see, says that genital sexual activity is only for procreation. Some current Roman Catholic thinking sees such activity not only for procreation but also as an expression of the love and union that exists between a man and wife. 'Sexual acts between members of the same sex are contrary not only to one of the purposes of the sexual faculty, namely, procreation, but also *to the other principle purpose* which is to express mutual love between husband and wife' (italics mine) – thus the National Conference of American Catholic Bishops' Publication *Principles to guide Confessors in questions of homosexuality*.[7] This is in line with the Natural Law argument used by Anglicans.

Here it would be argued that genital sexual intercourse 'in nature' is for the married couple – one man married to one woman for life. That is why adultery, fornication, homosexual relations and bestiality are wrong. What is 'in nature', as created by God, is 'the male and the female in heterosexual marriage', as Genesis 1–3 indicates. It is this totality of marriage which God has created and is 'in nature', not just sexual capability itself. Marriage is God's work and therefore his creation. He joins a man and a woman together (Mark 10:9), whether they realise it or not. Both Jesus and Paul spoke of marriage in terms of a 'gift'. This implies that it is not something 'achieved' (although it has to be worked at). It is not achieved either through procreation or through there being a 'good relationship'. It is not the relationship in either its sexual or social aspects that creates the marriage. It is more the marriage that creates the relationship. Thus marriage – the exclusive life commitment of one man for one woman, which society recognises and endorses – is the place for sexual activity. This is where human sexual development is leading. All this was gradually being learnt during the Old Testament period. It was Jesus himself who re-emphasised the basic principles regarding marriage.

It is not surprising, therefore, to find that it is in the light of marriage that every other sexual relationship and activity is judged. The primary sexual commandment relates to the preservation of the marriage bond – 'Thou shalt not commit adultery.' From this the rest follows.

This Anglican development of the appeal to Nature, now being echoed by Roman Catholics, does not see monogamy as just 'the institution best adapted to the care and education of children' (para 131). Rather it sees the monogamous relationship as a valuable thing in itself. It is a 'gift'. The procreation of children is more a consequence or the proper result, not the primary purpose of the marriage. The marriage is not defined by the fact of its children. Childless marriages are still marriages. Children are a resultant *blessing*. Sexual coitus can result in procreation. Its primary purpose is something much wider – the 'one-fleshment' of the man and the woman. If this was simply for procreation, it would put man on a level with the animals. But in Genesis 1, 'Sex difference is mentioned for the first time with the creation of man. It is as though it is only incidental to the rest of creation, but with man it has meaning.'[8]

This meaning is highlighted in genital sexual encounter

within and, as we can see, only within heterosexual marriage. This is not because each act is open to procreation, but because each act is at one and the same time an expressive realisation of personal commitment *and* potentially procreative. There are procreative possibilities. These not only lead to the need for contraception. (The biblical command to be fruitful and multiply is to be obeyed in a deliberate and human way, and not in an instinctive and animal way.) But they also give a rich significance to the act and enable it to be the expression and realisation of personal love that it is. Necessarily homosexual genital behaviour does not have these procreative possibilities. And as it falls outside the wider framework of the marriage bond it can be said to be against nature.

The homosexual condition
But we can ask questions with regard to 'Nature', not just about homosexual acts but also about the homosexual condition. The Gay Christian Movement itself uses Natural Law arguments here. This argument is 'that it is as natural for the homosexual person to be homosexual as for the heterosexual to be hetcrosexual' (para 141). Norman Pittinger, for example, can say that the 'natural law type of thought has value if it is re-interpreted to say that we should always act in accordance with our true nature'.[9]

Oliver O'Donovan, a former member of the Board for Social Responsibility, argues to the contrary. Our true nature is not what exists but what God intended. He argues that claims about nature for the Christian cannot be separated from the Doctrine of Creation, and then asks if God's creation of humanity is 'already divided into homosexual and heterosexual'.[10] The answer is 'No'. 'Like Judaism, Christianity has resisted the idea of original distinctions in the human race. Mankind is one kind ... almost all the significant differences among men, racial, cultural, and linguistic, are there (in the early chapters of Genesis) represented as supervening the Fall. Only one difference is

95

recorded before the Fall, the difference between male and female.' This is the simple heterosexual divide. The further divide into two types of humanity, one heterosexual and the other homosexual, is to be seen as fallen. God intended one heterosexual humanity. That, of course, does not allow us wrongly to penalise the homosexual condition – we are all fallen. And we need to heed Thielicke's words: 'The theologian who speaks of the dubious character of homosexuality – and he would be blind or forgetful of his mission if he ignored it – must in any case look at another side of the matter and dare not defame the *humanum* of the person so conditioned in order to make his negation easier.'[11]

Vocation

Another line of approach the Working Party employs to change the Biblical and traditional Christian ethic on homosexuality is to say that homosexuals 'cannot, therefore, enter into a heterosexual marriage . . . Yet they may not be called to celibacy and may long for that tenderness in genital relationships which heterosexuals can hope to experience in marriage' (para 164). Homosexuals, it is being said, are especially frustrated. Many heterosexuals cannot marry, true. 'But the frustration to which the homosexual man or woman is exposed is of a different order' (para 164). The conclusion soon comes in para 168: 'to declare that homosexuals may not in any circumstances give physical expression to their erotic love is unduly to circumscribe the area of responsible choice, to lay on individuals a burden too heavy for some to bear, and, by restricting the options open to them, to hinder their search for an appropriate way of life. In the light of some of the evidence we have received we do not think it possible to deny that there are circumstances in which individuals may justifiably choose to enter into a homosexual relationship with the hope of enjoying a companionship and physical expression of sexual love similar to that which is to be found in marriage' (para 168).

There is a fundamental confusion, surely, behind this. It

concerns the idea of 'vocation' or 'calling'. There is a suggestion in this part of the Report that there are only two callings – a calling to marriage, or a calling to celibacy, where celibacy is properly understood as a positive vocation, accepted as God's will for the achieving of his purpose – a eunuch for the kingdom of heaven's sake. Sexual abstinence is thus a means to a greater good, to which God is primarily calling the person. But does God never *call* us to sexual abstinence as a means of avoiding evil? Why can not this be seen as a calling, alongside marriage and celibacy 'actively embraced' (para 233)?

There is a calling of God in any and every situation for the Christian believer and that is his or her calling to be holy – 'the saints' (eg 1 Corinthians 1:2). And this has to be worked out in terms of 'negatives', from time to time – the things we should not do. We refrain from speaking, when words would harm. We refrain from going, when our presence would be unhelpful. And we refrain from doing, including sexual doing, when our actions would damage either individuals or society. But these 'abstinences' are part of our basic calling as God's people, a consequence of the calling to be holy.

In the New Testament Epistles the early Christians were often told to live out their calling by refraining from wrongdoing. A previous generation of theologians called this the 'mortification of the flesh'. It had a bad press from being misunderstood. It simply means, following Paul in Romans 8:13, that by the Spirit we are to 'put to death' all that is sinful in our lives. We do not do this in our own strength, but in God's. This is part of what it means to be called to be holy.

Furthermore in a situation of temptation we are assured of God's special strength as we seek to abstain from what is sinful. 'God is faithful, and he will not let you be tempted beyond your strength, but with the temptation will also provide the way of escape' (1 Corinthians 10:13).

This is the experience of Christians in both temptation

97

and testing. God's power is known. So wrote the authors of *The Problem of Homosexuality*: 'Precisely for those who find themselves in such moral perplexities is the grace of God available. It is a matter of Christian experience that faithful acceptance of a difficult way of life in response to a moral demand always finds reinforcement in a powerful movement from God towards man.'[12]

Marriage and human fulfilment

But how are we to think of marriage? Is it something which all men and women ought to enjoy? Yes and no. In the words of Richard Lovelace, 'In an unfallen world it might be true that every Adam would have an Eve.'[13] But the world is fallen. Some do not marry. God does not now call all to the married state. Therefore not all will be totally fulfilled sexually.

Nor is sexual fulfilment essential to true human fulfilment. It is possible to be human without being sexually fulfilled, although ancient fertility religions and their twentieth-century counterparts might seem to deny this. Sexual fulfilment is not to be made either into an idol or a demon. Christianity sees sexual fulfilment in altogether different categories. It is a gift whose meaning is only understood within the wider gift of marriage. *Nor is marriage essential to true human being.* This is the importance of Genesis 2, where Adam, the man (and the male) is truly human without his female. He is not 'fallen', although it is better for him to have a partner: 'It is not good that the man should be alone' (Genesis 2:18). Jesus, himself, supremely shows the truth of this. Jesus presents the fulfilled life; he demonstrates true human fulfilment as he is obedient to his father and lives for others. In one sense he was sexually unfulfilled. This does not imply *his* fallenness. True, in so far as he experienced 'aloneness', we can see this as his experiencing the pain of the world, which indeed was due to sin and the Fall. The Cross was the ultimate focus for that experience of 'aloneness' – 'My God, my God, why hast thou forsaken me?' (Mark 15:33). But on the Cross Jesus was truly human (and divine). Never more so. Here was total self-giving in love; the pinnacle of human expression. But it was not sexual.

We can, therefore, talk about God's ideal – marriage, which for many results in a call to be married. God's purpose for his kingdom, however, may be better achieved by some forgoing marriage. This results in a call to celibacy. But in the fallen world there are people who are not conscious of a 'vocation to celibacy'. Nor can they marry. But their call to holiness implies a call to abstinence.

The failure of the Working Party to make these various distinctions is no doubt due to their failure to come to grips with the concept of 'the Fall' itself. In para 151 there is an (unflattering) allusion to the early Church fathers: for them 'it was not that [sex] was inherently evil; but it was, since the Fall, disordered'. But there is no further discussion of the Fall. Yet it is impossible to have any concept of 'redemption' unless you have some concept of 'fallenness'.

Personalism

The Working Party Report adopts a 'personalist' approach to the solution of the homosexual problem. It finds the biblical evidence irrelevant, the traditional Natural Law approach (in the form it presents it) inadequate, but 'the personalist approach is able to do full justice to the conviction that sexuality is important, and provides a persuasive rationale for it, viz that sexual activity is the uniquely appropriate expression of profound erotic love between the sexes (and, perhaps, between those who are erotically attracted, whatever their sex)' (para 146).

What is a personalist approach? Is it credible? Does it lead to the acceptance of homosexual relationships?

In one sense the gospel *is* 'personalist'. It is about persons, it is about God's love for men and women, not just 'structures'. 'The Sabbath was made for man, not man for the Sabbath.' No-one can deny the primacy of the person in one sense. But how does the Gay Christian Movement or some of its spokesmen see the primacy of the person? This is important. The Working Party admitted that 'much of the evidence we received on behalf of homosexual equality was given from a personalist standpoint' (para 140) and this was described as 'persuasive testimony', and 'in the light of some of the evidence we have received we do not think it possible to deny that there are circumstances in which individuals may justifiably choose to enter into a homosexual relationship' (para 168).

Norman Pittinger is I suppose, the most distinguished of the Gay Christian Movement's theologians. He puts matters thus: 'Let me say frankly that I believe that any and all sexual activity, genital or otherwise, is good – provided that it does not violate the intentional understanding of each other human as a person and not simply and solely as a *thing*. Some of us would be prepared to say that the "one night stand" for instance, cannot be called evil in itself; there is genuine goodness there, in so far as loneliness is overcome, some slight sense of companionship is given, strong desire is released and to some degree satisfied.'[14] As a summary of his position he says this: 'Before I conclude, I must spell out a little more precisely the implication of what I have called "thingifying" as morally wrong in sexual contexts. I have often remarked that the question which might well be asked by any of us, after a genital (or approximately genital) experience, is this: "Am I now leaving a body which has given me great satisfaction *or* am I now leaving a person with whom I have enjoyed an enhancement of life?"' '[15]

In part, well and good. People should not be used as objects. People matter more than things and should be respected. But the fallacy in personalism lies in seeing only *one* dichotomy, the dichotomy between behaviour that is personal, and behaviour that 'thingifies' (to use Pittinger's word). There is however another dichotomy, the dichotomy between selfish and selfless behaviour. and the two dichotomies are not the same. Personalists tend to assume that they are the same, or forget the latter. So, Pittinger can say 'Lust, I insist is good; after all, it is only deep desire, as its old English usage indicates. But *sinful* lust is desire which cannot see anything worth desiring save the strictly genital.'[16] Desire is sinful, he says, in virtue of its failure to see a 'person'. It only sees that person as a thing to be played with. But of course desire is sinful when it is *selfish*. The way of Christ is the way of self-denial, and true love is sacrificial where a man is prepared to lay down his life for his friends. It is not defined as seeing those friends simply as persons.

Alex Davidson, writing as a homosexual, has a good commentary on the personalist fallacy. Referring to sexual and genital needs he writes to his male friend, '(These) other wants are related, of course, but what I want most is *you*, not as a plaything or as a picture, but as a person. Now this, whispers the tempter earnestly, is much less carnal, much more lofty a sentiment. Yes, say I, but equally selfish, still wanting, still demanding ... I like to claim that I could draw the line between the "loftier" ... and the more "carnal" ... (but) the operative word on both sides of the line is desire, and the attitude throughout is "I want".'[17]

The morality of sexual activity is not, for the Christian, a matter of whether it 'personalises', but rather whether it achieves God's intention, namely the 'one-fleshment' of the husband and wife. Nor do Christian ethics put too high a stress on 'the personal', defined in quasi 'spiritual' terms of relationships, as is often done by those who argue for a relaxing of the Christian sexual code. No, in Hebrew and Christian thought the person is robustly physical. Within the marriage bond there is a place for the 'strictly genital', a pure enjoyment of sexuality. Indeed there is a proper place for the sensuous, as is made clear in the Song of Solomon. Within the marriage covenant, to which the two parties have selflessly given themselves 'for better for worse', pure mutual bodily enjoyment is one of those things which seals as well as signifies the covenant. Because the couple are already in a 'personal relationship' they have the freedom to enjoy each other's physicality – there is no need constantly to be asking 'am I treating you as a person?' The proper question to ask is, 'Am I treating you as my wife or husband?' The Bible suggests that included in that question is another: 'Am I selflessly letting you enjoy my body?' (cf 1 Corinthians 7:3–5).

'Context' and love

The personalist argument appears to go hand in hand with a situationalist argument. Some of those 'from a personalist standpoint' who gave 'persuasive testimony' to the Working Party 'complained about what seemed to them an over-emphasis upon various genital acts', whereas, they claimed, for many homosexual people themselves these are secondary and what counts is the relationship as a whole (para 140). Here is a desire to focus on the context not the act. If the context or 'situation' is good or loving, then the act is good or loving.

But the trouble with this line of thinking is twofold. First, it often forgets that the context or situation in terms of which it judges specific actions is itself within a wider context or situation. A genital homosexual act does not just take place within the context of a relationship between two men or women. It also takes place within the context of the total community within which that relationship is one part. The Christian then argues that the total community exists within the context of God's love and ordering. If he has made it clear that certain behaviour is wrong, we cannot but take note. For we realise that God's ordering is an ordering of love; we see these prohibitions not as restrictive but as the path to true goodness and genuine love.

Secondly, this line of thinking often fails to examine the notion of 'love' in the light of the New Testament. But such an examination is especially necessary today when the term can frequently conceal a basic selfishness which is fundamentally opposed to the generous self-giving which is signified by the New Testament word *agapē*. As David

102

Field has written: 'Replacing all other absolute standards by the single command to love is not only unfaithful to the New Testament teaching. It is also patently inadequate as an un-supported prop for moral vision in the best of us.' He quotes the former Archbishop of Canterbury, Michael Ramsey, 'It is on a deductive theory from the concept of love, and not upon a full examination of Christ's teaching, that the conclusion is being drawn that "nothing of itself can be labelled wrong".'[18]

Jesus, of course, taught the need for love. Jesus stressed the need for inward attitudes and motives to be right. Motives are necessary. But they are not sufficient. Good motives do not make bad actions good. Peter no doubt had good motives when he tried to oppose Jesus in his readiness to face death in Jerusalem. Jesus, nevertheless, turned to Peter and said, 'Get behind me, Satan! For you are not on the side of God but of men.'

NOTES

1 *Report of the Committee on Homosexual Offences and Prostitution*, op cit, p 16, 32
2 Roger Moss, op cit, p 29
3 *The Problem of Homosexuality*, op cit, p 15
4 H. C. G. Moule, *Charles Simeon* (London, 1948) p 79
5 D. S. Bailey, op cit p 157
6 Richard F. Lovelace, op cit, pp 111–12
7 *Principles to Guide Confessors in Questions of Homosexuality* (Washington: 1973) p 3
8 C. G. Scorer, *Life in our hands* (Inter-Varsity Press, Leicester: 1978) p 61–62
9 Norman Pittinger, *Some notes on an ethic for homosexuals* (Working Paper 1, Gay Christian Movement)
10 O. M. T. O'Donovan, *Is it a natural alternative?* in *Insight*, June 1978, The Bulletin of Wycliffe College, Toronto
11 Helmut Thielicke, op cit, p 271
12 *The Problem of Homosexuality*, op cit, p 15
13 Richard F. Lovelace, op cit, p 84

14 Norman Pittinger, op cit.
15 Ibid
16 Ibid
17 Alex Davidson, op cit, p 79
18 David Field, *The Homosexual Way* (Inter-Varsity Press, Leicester: 1979) p 32–33

6 LAW AND GRACE

Every discussion on homosexuality has to face the fact that there is a political dimension to it. Homosexuality affects the 'polis' – the wider community. This is why it becomes the concern of the law, which deals with 'the relationship between the homosexual minority and the wider society of which it forms a part' (para 172).

But is the Church to be concerned with the law? Is not that 'Caesar's' business? These are good questions to be asking in view of the increasing politicisation of the Church. It is certainly true that the duty of the Church is to preach the gospel, not declare the law. The Church in some ways begins where the law leaves off. The law is a schoolmaster to bring us to Christ. But there are good and bad schoolmasters!

However, once the gospel is proclaimed and received there *must* be social results, *if* it has been truly preached and truly believed. Sooner or later there will have to be some involvement on the part of Christian people in the political arena. No doubt when it comes to the detailed business of law making there will be legitimate differences of opinion among Christians as to what is appropriate. If the law is both to curb the worst excesses of human sin and to give some moral guidance, and if this is to be done in the light of reality (the hardness of men's hearts) the problems are obvious.

But when we turn to the Bible, what was the distinctive role of God's spokesmen when they dealt with politics? It was not to advise on legal compromises, but to give an evaluation of the political whole – the whole spectrum of life in the community – from God's point of view. The prophets did not get involved with Ahab or Ahaz in some political deal. They spoke of the much broader themes of 'justice, kindness and walking humbly with God' (Micah 6:8). They asked questions of the state. Was it exhibiting those two necessary ingredients of righteousness (a stronger term than our 'justice') and mercy (a stronger term than our 'kindness')? Above all did it acknowledge the God of righteousness and mercy?

Homosexuality and culture

How then does homosexuality affect the wider society? Tom Driver in an article entitled *Homosexuality: the Contemporary and Christian Contexts*, argues that the Gay Liberation Movement has raised homosexuality to the level of political consciousness. 'As a result we can no longer deal with it as if it were merely a psychological problem or a question of private morality; rather it is now a question of public policy.'[1] This is in line with Kate Millett's postscript to her best seller *Sexual Politics*. She there concludes: 'The enormous social change involved in a sexual revolution is basically a matter of altered consciousness, the exposure and elimination of social and psychological realities underlining political and cultural structures. We are speaking, then, of a cultural revolution.'[2]

But there is nothing especially new or radical here. 'A disintegration of sexual morals will affect deleteriously all the other ingredients of our civilisation: its emphasis on the significance of persons, its rule of law against arbitrary power, its disinterested science, its literature and art, even its reasons for rebellion, for rebellion has to have a norm to withstand.'[3] So wrote a distinguished member of the Wolfenden Committee, the former Regius Professor of Pastoral and Moral Theology in the University of Oxford, V. A. Demant. He reminds us that it was the great Russian philosopher, Berdyaev, who saw the real significance of the value of sexual restraint for society.

Sexual restraint is a vital aspect of man's mastery of

nature which has been the great contribution of Western civilisation to the world. 'Part of that mastery over nature in man's own life has been a mastery over the sexual impulse, to a degree in European Christendom not known elsewhere. But it has been known or practised to some degree throughout mankind's civilised history. All cultural development has meant a limitation of sexual drives. B. Malinowski in his *Sex and Repression in Savage Society* shows that even an elementary culture demands some limit on sexual adventure.'[4]

For us, as we think about the wider implications of homosexuality, it is the rejection of the absolute sanctity of heterosexual marriage that is significant. Were this to be accepted, even in small measure, it would have social, cultural and therefore 'political' implications. In some Gay Christian circles this attack is serious. Bill Johnson, a practising American homosexual minister can say. 'As long as the Church is able to perpetuate the belief that marriage and the family are the highest form of human relationship it will be able to perpetuate itself as a heterosexual family-orientated institution ... heterosexual relationships and marriage as traditionally experienced are basically unhealthy.'[5] This is a fully Gay Liberation Front position. In the revised (1979) Gay Liberation Front manifesto we are told, 'We must aim at the abolition of the family.'[6] And the buttress of the family? – Christianity: 'Christianity, whose archaic and irrational teachings support the family and marriage as the only permitted condition for sex.'[7] No doubt many less extreme homosexuals want to live and let live. They do not want to destroy other people's families. But to affirm the homosexual way as an alternative, even in the way the Working Party does, is to do something radical to the social consciousness as it affects the family.

There is evidence that in the Gay Christian Movement there is a move towards the Gay Liberation position. Indeed a recent book by key members of the Gay Christian Movement is entitled *Towards a Theology of Gay Liberation*. In it Malcolm Macourt, its editor, first argues against the view that homosexuals are born and not made, the view that there is a ' "true homosexual" (that marvellous creation of the 1950's reformers created to assist in the removal of the more gory anti-gay legal and social restrictions)'.[8] Then he argues for a *free and random* model of behaviour. The 'ideal' is where you have the free choice between a number of options in a society 'in which young people, as they grow up, will become aware of a wide variety of life patterns: monogamy – multiple partnerships; partnerships for life – partnerships for a period of mutual growth; same-sex partners – opposite sex partners – both; chastity; living in community – living in small family units; and so on. A world, furthermore, where each young person becomes aware that each of these life patterns is held in equal esteem in society. So that each will feel free to choose the pattern or partners with whom they wish to share their lives – to choose the person or persons with whom it *makes most sense* to them to live.'[9] This is the vision of the gay liberationists. The Christian gay liberationist will choose a pattern which 'makes most sense' in a way that allows him to love God and to love his neighbour. But this is consistent, apparently, with any kind of sexual pairing.

We have argued earlier how impossible and wrong such a position is for the Christian.

The law

There is, then, the possibility of radical cultural and social change through an increase in homosexual behaviour. Maybe the traditional conclusion drawn from the Sodom story that homosexuality has damaging political consequences has some truth in it. But certainly this possibility will mean that it is not improper for the law to have a direct concern in the question of homosexuality. Professor Basil Mitchell, one of the members of the Working Party, has written elsewhere, echoing Lord Devlin, that 'the law has a right to protect the institutions that are judged essential to a

given society and the morality associated with them ...
Among the institutions in our society to which the law gives
protection is the monogamous family and it is here that
there is room for a degree of moral paternalism.'[10]

But the law is not only protective. It does have influence
even though it cannot enforce morality. What is legal soon
comes to be understood as what is right. It would not be
surprising if a report of one American psychiatrist is true. It
is claimed that since homosexual practices were legalised in
his state, he has not been able to cure any homosexual
patients, whereas previously he had had some success.[11]
This is consistent with the need for people to be motivated if
they are to be changed.

Perhaps for these reasons the present law has value. The
Working Party is aware that there is now 'a major campaign
aimed at securing further change in the law as to homosexual conduct' (para 187). The Working Party is supporting the movement for reform in certain areas. It
supports the idea of a new offence of 'offensive sexual behaviour in public view'. If the Law Commissioners' draft
Bill were passed a homosexual (or heterosexual) person
would be guilty of an offence, for having sexual intercourse
or some other form of sexual behaviour, 'if he does so in
such circumstances that he knows or ought to know that his
conduct is likely to be seen by other persons to whom it is
likely to cause serious offence' (clause 21, draft Bill in Law
Com No 76).

But perhaps something more is needed than merely the
notion of 'offensive' behaviour. This could be included. But
'offensiveness' must not stand alone. The Criminal Law Act
1977 s 5 (3) speaks of behaviour which 'tends to corrupt
public morals or outrages public decency'. The Wolfenden
Committee had spoken of the need 'to preserve public order
and decency' as well. Many, indeed, might not be 'offended'
by overt homosexual (or heterosexual) behaviour, but they
still might judge it to be indecent, improper or destructive of
public order. 'Offensiveness' is more a judgement of the

feelings or emotions. These are affected or modified by exposure to what 'offends'. In time, for example, one ceases to be 'offended' by sexual display on newstalls, in the cinema and on the stage. But one still judges it to be indecent or improper or destructive of public order and public morals. This is a judgement as to what is appropriate or fitting and conducive to the good of society. It depends on intellectual as well as emotional criteria. Any new law surely needs to take account of this. Too often it is assumed by some that persons with a concern for 'public order and decency' are also those who are 'squeamish' or 'offended' or 'disgusted' over sexual matters. This is not necessarily true. Many simply judge that public sexual display is in fact unhealthy; they do not have strong 'feelings' about it. If there is any emotion it is more often than not one of sadness rather than disgust. They would still judge, however, that it was not in the interests of 'public order'.

The Working Party supports the Law Commission in its recommendation to abolish common law conspiracy and other common law offences relating to 'the corruption of public morals or outrage of public decency'. (It was in its review of common law conspiracy that the Law Commission proposed a new offence of 'offensive sexual behaviour in public view'.) This is technical, but the relevant point for us is that the passing of the 1967 Act meant that homosexual activities were no longer directly punishable by the criminal law. But this did not imply that the law no longer considered them to be corrupting practices. 'As Lord Reid expressed it in *Knuller v DPP* (the *International Times* case, 1973), "I find nothing ... to indicate that Parliament thought or intended to lay down that indulgence in [homosexual] practices is not corrupting. I read the Act as saying that, even though they may be corrupting, if people choose to corrupt themselves in this way, that is their affair and the law will not interfere. But no licence is given to others to encourage the practice." ' (para 192).

The result of all this is that someone who is judged to be

110

promoting homosexual activity technically is at risk under common law at present. That is why the Working Party supports the abolition of these common law offences. For they say 'there are difficulties for *bona fide* counselling and supportive organisations for homosexual people . . . (they) fear criminal prosecution by the use of one of the common law offences'. The Working Party refers to the organisers of homosexual clubs and groups. It admits that such clubs 'can be an undesirable stimulus to promiscuous sexual activity', but 'these dangers must be put alongside the very real benefits such organisations may confer' (para 194).

What do we say? First, in terms of the law, the common law of conspiracy has been virtually abolished by the Criminal Law Act 1977; but there are certain important exceptions. These were deliberately made and they include 'entering into an agreement to engage in conduct which tends to corrupt public morals or outrages public decency' (Criminal Law Act 1977 s 5 (1)). This exception is a legal safety-net. New offences covering this and related offences no doubt could be created, as the Law Commission suggests. But it would need to be ensured that what common law rightly prohibits is still prohibited. Such action would then 'not of course involve any abdication by the state of its role as a guardian of public morals' (para 193) – something the Working Party obviously believes to be important.

Secondly, one criminologist has written: 'The law of conspiracy has been a favourite target for criticism, but some offence of conspiracy to corrupt public morals does seem a desirable safeguard. Nor do I see why homosexual counsellors should have any more to fear from the law here than probation officers or social workers need to fear being prosecuted for conspiring, aiding, abetting, counselling, procuring or inciting to commit burglary!'[12] He points out that the crucial factor is the nature of the official advice. Those gay organisations which promote homosexual activity are at risk, and should be. But it is extremely unlikely that organisations like the True Freedom Trust which follow a Chris-

111

tian ethic in homosexual counselling would ever be in danger from the law.

Thirdly, this raises the alleged value of these clubs. The psychiatrist Montague Barker, in the Christian Medical Fellowship pamphlet on homosexuality has said 'Gay clubs only serve to exploit the homosexual by reinforcing his homosexual feelings and behaviour and limiting his social contacts to other homosexuals. A much better approach is to draw him into a more mixed society and thus enable him to acquire wider identifications.'[13]

The Working Party then goes on to advocate a lowering of the age of consent with regard to homosexual practices. At present, twenty-one is the age of consent. Homosexual acts with those under twenty-one are still punishable at law. The Working Party is in favour of a reduction in the age to eighteen (para 202).

However, the Working Party reminds us that 'one member of the Wolfenden Committee, the Marquess of Lothian, has recently expressed his opposition to the lowering of the age from twenty-one to eighteen. He was speaking in the debate in the House of Lords 14 June 1977 which ended in the rejection by 146 votes (including the three bishops present) to 25 of a Bill designed to make that change in the law. Lord Lothian's view was that the 18–21 age group was still at risk of exploitation, and he referred to a medical view that many young men do not establish a definite gender role until they are between those ages' (para 201). The Working Party then goes on to say in para 203, 'The crucial point in the argument is whether or not there is a significant number of young men aged between eighteen and twenty-one who are at risk ... The Working Party does not believe that there is.' No arguments, however, are given for their 'belief'.

There are indeed a number of people at universities or at the start of certain careers where there is a significant risk. Indeed since 1973 the National Union of Students has been actively promoting the gay cause. That year there was an

112

NUS conference resolution that 'the gay cause is one of civil rights and social change; but the problems of homosexuals will not be solved by mere tolerance. Improvement in the social standing of homosexuals entails positive acceptance rather than condescension. The total integration of homosexuals and other minority groups requires fundamental change in society.' Leonard Barnett writes: 'The importance of the resolution was to be seen also in the proposals for practical on going action. The instructions to local branches of the NUS throughout the country included practical suggestions aimed at improving the situation of the gay student by active support of gay organisations and alliance with others campaigning for law reform; and *the establishment and encouragement of gay societies at colleges and universities*' (italics mine).[14]

Anyone familiar with university common-rooms, halls of residence and students' unions will know of the enormous 'pressure' that there has recently been from the gay caucus. This does create a risk. The age of consent, surely, should remain at twenty-one. Kinsey reported a drop in the amount of homosexual behaviour between the ages of twenty-one and twenty-five. His conclusion was that 'during their late teens, many males experience considerable personal conflict over their homosexual activities ... and try to make the heterosexual adjustments which society demands.' Some are successful. Some are not. But orientation is settled as far as Kinsey is concerned 'somewhere in their middle twenties'.[15] This needs to be noted even if we are sceptical about Kinsey's method of selecting cases. This is true of known homosexuals.

Minority rights and paedophilia
The Working Party admits that the 'homosexual minority' is not entitled to 'full equality in social, educational and theological terms' (para 175). It is no doubt wise to look at each 'claim' individually, as the Working Party does. But on what criterion are rights given to minorities? Does being a

113

minority in a community automatically confer special rights? This is often assumed. Of course there are fundamental human rights and freedoms which need to be accorded to all. Indeed in society there are criminal minorities (also with their own organisations) – they have rights. But not the right to function in any way they please. Limitations to freedom obviously are imposed when others are affected or involved. As Lord Reid said, 'If people choose to corrupt themselves ... that is their own affair ... But no licence is given to others to encourage the practice' (see p 110).

This question becomes acute as we consider the 'rights' of the minority committed to paedophilia (the sexual love of an adult for a child). The Working Party seems to be arguing for the abolition of the common law offence relating to public morals and public decency to facilitate the work of supportive groups for paedophiles as well as homosexuals: 'Although a homosexual club can promote a ghetto mentality, and can be an undesirable stimulus to promiscuous sexual activity, these dangers must be put alongside the very real benefits such organisations may confer. Similar arguments can be applied to groups arranged by or for those attracted by young children' (para 194).

The Working Party wants to argue that the individual homosexual man or woman is no more likely to be attracted to the young than is the individual heterosexual man or woman, so there is no link between homosexuality and paedophilia. Furthermore it denies that 'propaganda on behalf of paedophilia' is linked 'with the campaign for a more sympathetic understanding of homosexuality'. This may be true. At its Sheffield conference in 1975 the Campaign for Homosexual Equality was reported as only voting to develop 'an informed perspective' on paedophilia.[16] But the question then has to be asked not about propaganda but support. Is *support* for homophile organisations associated with *support* for paedophile organisations, and is *sympathy* for paedophilia linked with *sympathy* for homosexuality? The Christian surely would want to support and sympathise

114

with the *person* who had paedophile (or homosexual) problems, but vigorously oppose as wrong and harmful both paedophilia itself (and homosexual practices) and any organisations which encourage such behaviour. In the New Testament we see that Jesus opposed disease itself, but had compassion on the sick.

Family life and friendship
After the Working Party has dealt with these legal matters in chapter five, 'A Legal Perspective on Homosexuality', it comes in chapter six to 'Social Implications and Pastoral Care'.

First it makes certain points about social life, related to some of the things we have discussed already. In para 224 the Working Party refers to the fear 'that homosexuality as such represents a serious threat to the conception of the family'. In para 225 it says: 'We believe that this fear is largely unjustified. It presupposes a wider extension of homosexual practices among the great majority of people whose predominant disposition is not homosexual.'

But Kinsey has shown how often homosexual activity is engaged in by those whose predominant disposition is not homosexual. Then as we have seen earlier (p 62), homosexual practices appear to be culturally conditioned. Their incidence varies from society to society. Furthermore Kinsey indicated that the incidence of homosexual practice varies in terms of educational attainment and it varies between the country and the town.[17]

There is thus every evidence that patterns of homosexual behaviour can and do change according to environmental factors. The thesis of Malcolm Macourt of the Gay Christian Movement is that we simply *can* choose. If more people are persuaded of that, it is perfectly possible for homosexual practices to spread.

One other important social matter is dealt with in chapter six – friendship. It quite rightly draws attention to the fact that if homosexual unions were accepted more freely, this would impose a significant strain on persons of the same sex who wanted to live together perfectly normally and without any genital activity at all. 'It would be unfortunate if the "liberalisation" of society in regard to homosexuality resulted in close friendships being automatically interpreted as involving genital expression' (para 232). But having raised this problem, no solution is suggested by the Working Party.

Pastoral concerns

The fundamental Christian contribution to the homosexual question is not in terms of law, but in terms of grace. The gospel to the homosexual is not 'Don't', but 'God loves you and wants to help you'. God can bring change. Not necessarily precisely as we always want or expect it, but in accordance with his will which is always good and perfect. William Temple once said that it is quite untrue to say that human nature cannot be changed, for that is precisely why God sent his son into the world, to be its Saviour and why the Holy Spirit came to make that salvation effective.

However, in this section of the Report dealing with pastoral matters, the Board for Social Responsibility in its Critical Observations noted with sadness a neglect of 'those distinctive features which Christian theology imposes upon Christian pastoral care. In particular there is no consideration of sin and forgiveness in an area of life in which it is likely to be a real issue' (para A19).

But the principles of pastoral care are spelt out. It is said that the goal of the pastor is to enable each person to reach a 'conscientious decision', which 'once made should be respected'. This is to be based on Christian values. 'The values to be taken into account should include that expressed by the traditional virtue of "chastity", where chastity is understood to signify *not necessarily total abstinence from sexual activity*, but certainly its subordination to the deeper and more inclusive demands of personal relationships' (para 246 – italics mine).

This is confused. The mere fact that decisions are made in

'good conscience' is irrelevant as to whether those decisions are right or wrong. Conscience may have to be educated. What the Christian pastor, surely, should say is that the *person* should be respected while his decisions, if wrong, should be opposed by prayer and argument. But 'opposition' is not the same as 'overriding'. Respect for the person rules out the pastor overriding a person's decision. Love, however, demands an attempt to put right what is wrong or self-damaging.

None of this is a problem for the Christian. The humanist values man in virtue of his decisions and choices. His significance comes from his choices in life. These tend to become sacrosanct. The Christian can believe a man's decisions to be hopelessly wrong but still give him value, because he is made 'in the image and likeness of God'.

Therefore it is questionable whether 'the primary task of the Christian pastor is to enable him or her to reach such a (conscientious) decision' (para 246). The primary task of the pastor is to enable the person by counselling to reach a decision which is according to the will of God, rather than to his or her own whim or fancy or 'free and random model'. This does not mean being insensitive to personal integrity. Indeed, when there is no free decision the pastoral goal will not have been reached. How this goal is reached may be by directive or non-directive methods.

The Church and the homosexual

What should the Church's reaction be in general as it considers ministry to the homosexual? Richard Lovelace has some wise words on this: 'In order for both pastors and lay people to minister effectively to gays, the Christian Church will be forced to come to terms with its own inner attitudes and feelings towards the whole issue of sexuality. These are currently out of balance in either of two polar directions: *permissiveness* and *repression*.'[18]

There needs to be clear teaching about the biblical view of sexuality and homosexuality. The Church then needs to teach about freedom. The Bible shows us that freedom is a privilege that God has given to man. Man does not live by instinct but by free choice. This is true of his sexual life, even when (or if) he or she has a homosexual orientation. There is the choice 'not to'. Man's choice can be according to God's will or against it. When it is against it, it leads to frustration, confusion and disorder. And this can be the case in the Church.

When there is sexual confusion in the Church, what is to be the Christian's response? The Church at Corinth is a good example of a church where there was sexual confusion. In 1 Corinthians 5 there is cited the case of a man acting irregularly from a sexual point of view. He was sleeping with his father's wife, and was presumably impenitent and continuing the relationship. We do not find that Paul asked whether the man was having a loving or fulfilling relationship with his father's wife. What we find is that the apostle demanded that the man should be disciplined. The details of that disciplining are not clear. But it was treated as a serious matter.

Many today believe that the credibility of the Church is at stake. This is no more so than in the case of avowed and practising homosexual clergy. The clergyman is to be an 'example to the flock' (1 Peter 5:3); he is to be 'above reproach, the husband of one wife, temperate, sensible, dignified ... moreover he must be well thought of by outsiders' (1 Timothy 3:2 and 7). No practising homosexual clergyman should be allowed to remain in office. There needs to be discipline.

But there needs to be the gospel. The gospel is that we *all*, homosexuals and heterosexuals alike, are in need of forgiveness, healing (in some part of our lives), and empowering. All three needs are inter-related. Often we need to be assured that our guilt is forgiven and our fears released before we can move forward in the direction that God is leading us. The Cross of Jesus is the place of forgiveness. As we see that Christ died for us we can be assured of God's acceptance and then experience new life in the power of the Holy Spirit.

The heart of the gospel is just here – that God loves us and accepts us, just as we are, with all our hang-ups, dispositions, experiences and histories. We do not have to make ourselves 'good' before he accepts us. No, we simply need to open our eyes to his love. But God's love is warm. Like a fire it both gives us new heart and burns up (or begins to) all that is evil in our lives. Thus the evidence that we have really opened to God's love is change. 'If the Spirit of him who raised Jesus from the dead dwells in you, he who raised Christ Jesus from the dead will give life to your mortal bodies also through his Spirit which dwells in you' (Romans 8:11). That is a promise, it is fulfilled at Christ's return. But it begins to be fulfilled now. Some will inherit the promise through faith and patience. For others there is more immediate experience. But the ultimate truth is that 'in all these things we are more than conquerors' (Romans 8:37). The battles are hard. 'But the homosexual who is not relieved of his *condition* will always find the Holy Spirit's aid to control his conduct.'[19]

Conclusion
How can we summarise what ought to be the Church's stand regarding homosexuality? First, we need to make it quite clear that we distinguish homosexual tendencies from homosexual activity. We then need to make it quite clear that people with homosexual tendencies, possibly through no fault of their own, and who do not engage in homosexual activity, are, of course, to be fully accepted in the Church without criticism, but rather with support. More will be said about this in Part III. It is not temptation that is wrong; after all, Jesus was tempted. It is giving in to temptation that is wrong.

Secondly, we have to say that homosexual activity is wrong and sinful, and needs forgiveness, but forgiveness is freely available in Christ, as we repent and confess our sins.

119

Thirdly, we *all* sin, and none of us can put ourselves on pedestals. Heterosexual people who criticise homosexual people may be far worse sinners in other areas of their lives. Homosexual sin is not the worst sin in the book! Jesus said it would 'be more tolerable . . . for Sodom' at the judgement than for communities (probably respectable communities) which reject his word and his workers (Luke 10:12).

Fourthly, in Jesus Christ there is not only forgiveness for sin, but also healing and that includes healing for the homosexual. This healing takes many forms. We look now at one specific case.

NOTES

1 Quoted in John J. McNeill, op cit, p 4
2 Kate Millett, *Sexual Politics* (Virago, London: 1977) p 362
3 V. A. Demant, *An exposition of Christian Sex Ethics* (London: 1963) pp 94–95
4 Ibid p 100
5 Quoted in Richard F. Lovelace, op cit p 46
6 *Gay Liberation Front Manifesto* (London: 1979) p 7
7 Ibid p 2
8 Malcom Macourt, *Towards a Theology of Gay Liberation* (SCM, London: 1977) p 26
9 Ibid p 25
10 Basil Mitchell, *Law, Morality and Religion in a Secular Society* (OUP, London: 1970) pp 67–68
11 Cited by C. W. Haskell in his pamphlet *Homosexuality and the Christian*
12 J. D. C. Harte, Lecturer in Law, University of Newcastle upon Tyne
13 Montague G. Barker, *Homosexuality* (CMF, Guidelines No 59) p 5
14 Leonard Barnett, *Homosexuality: Time to tell the truth* (Gollancz, London: 1975) p 123–24
15 A. C. Kinsey (*et al*) op cit p 629–30
16 Reported in *Sheffield Morning Telegraph* 21 August 1975
17 A. C. Kinsey (*et al*) op cit pp 482 and 630
18 Richard F. Lovelace, op cit, p 128
19 David Field, op cit p 36

7 A PROFILE

How does all this work out in real life? It is all very well reaffirming the biblical (and traditional) view on homosexual relationships, but is it practical? Part III of this book goes into some more detail; but this part concludes with the transcription of an interview with a young man, now living and working in the North East. He is someone who would claim that the love and power of Christ as witnessed to in Scripture are available for today and the guidelines of Scripture are still relevant.

When we met, I first began by asking him when it was that he discovered he was homosexual.

MT I first realised that I was homosexual when I was about twelve.

DH But how did you at twelve identify yourself as homosexual? People would argue that everyone goes through a homosexual phase around that time.

MT Well, I was obviously becoming sexually aware and I just made the basic discovery that I was more attracted to men than to women. At the time I didn't know it was called 'being homosexual'; I simply found men exciting. I knew what attracted me physically and sexually.

But I was quite a lonely person; and partly through being homosexual I felt rejected and different to other people, and partly through where I lived – I didn't live near anybody who went to school with me – I felt quite isolated. What really drew me to Christ in the first place was the warmth of the Christian fellowship in a youth club of a lively church. The people really were different and they were so friendly; that made all the difference.

121

It didn't take much to make me become a Christian, because they had something I wanted. So I became a Christian when I was fifteen and a half. (My parents weren't church-goers at all.)

DH But you had a secret homosexual relationship in the church with someone who was a professing Christian.

MT That's right.

DH How long did it last?

MT It lasted for two years. But right from the beginning I'd had my doubts and uncertainties. It all stemmed from our being very, very close friends. We got on well together, and helped each other spiritually, at first. Then he approached me sexually. I was totally mixed up, but because I respected him on lots of other matters, I decided I would respect him on his view of homosexuality.

DH You hadn't had a fully sexual homosexual relationship before that?

MT No.

DH What age were you, when this happened?

MT Nearly seventeen.

DH How old was your partner?

MT He was quite a bit older than myself. We had a sexual relationship for two years; over that time I often wondered about it all, but in many ways I did find it a fulfilling relationship. He especially did. He found it extremely fulfilling and would count those two years as a time of great spiritual growth and encouragement. But it eventually got to the stage for myself, in the second year, when I was finding it harder and harder in my own Christian life. Even then, I couldn't see that it was my homosexual relationship that was ruining my spiritual life. So it was almost just as a test that I asked – and this was very difficult to do – if we could finish the sexual side of things for a while, for me to get myself sorted out. It was very hard for both of us, but he, obviously, agreed. I found it such a relief that I

122

knew I had done the right thing, and that it was the relationship which had been holding me back in my Christian life. And so actually coming out of the relationship was a great step forward for me.

DH At this time did your parents know that this was going on?

MT No. They were very blind never to have realised. They never said anything. Then I had my first year at the University of Durham. I thought a little bit over the homosexual question there, and I was really struck by the argument from Creation about man being made for woman and vice versa; but I didn't think a lot about it. Then it was during my summer holidays, after my first year, that I went through a time of being not terribly, but a bit depressed and rather lonely. So I went back to my partner really to have another shot at the relationship, to see if it could work this time. I was very hopeful that he would meet my loneliness, and that we could actually make it work before God, this next time. But almost immediately I knew that it wouldn't be so, and that we couldn't start again anyway in our relationship. In fact we were straight back to where we always had been.

But during my second year at the University, for the first time the Lord really began to convict me about the place I was giving to the Holy Spirit in my life; and one of the areas – there were three main areas that the Lord was pointing at – one of them was homosexuality. It wasn't that I should abstain from homosexual relationships – well it was that, but it wasn't *just* that. What God was actually demanding was that he should be in full control of my total sexuality, no matter what it was. God was saying that he wanted to be in charge of it and that if I wanted to experience the Lordship of Christ and the fullness of the Spirit, then that would come through surrendering my sexuality to him. And part of that would mean giving up homosexual practices. It was only a part. But that's what I wanted from God and so I was quite prepared for this surrender and quite happy about it. It was almost immediately afterwards that I began to share with my closest friends that I was homosexual.

DH So by now, you had become aware that homosexual practice was not God's will.

MT Oh yes. I was convinced of that.

DH At what stage were you convinced?

MT Well, in a way I would say I'd always had an inkling that that's the way it was. All the time that I'd been a Christian, I'd had so many doubts about my relationship with my partner. During my first year at Durham, this thing about the Creation story really did strike me; it really hit home, although it didn't immediately change what I actually did. It was during the second year and leading up to the time that I was filled with the Spirit that I became absolutely convinced, in such a way that I can't believe I'll ever change my mind again on the matter. So I suppose that's when things were really clinched. And that's when I lost all fear of being known as being 'gay'. I also began to feel a real desire to help other gay people. During my second year I was slowly coming out to one or two people – friends – and talking to them. Then during my third year at University I wrote an article on Christianity and homosexuality for our College magazine. In this I specifically said that I was a homosexual but believed that it was wrong to practise as such and that God could help and was helping me.

DH You talk about 'a real desire to help other gay people'. How do you begin with someone in the gay Christian scene? You yourself talk about 'healing'. But many would deny they need 'healing'; many would deny that there is anything wrong with them – the trouble is the community around. It doesn't recognise them as being a legitimate and in one sense 'straight' part. It's the

124

community that's crooked. What is your own kind of approach and ministry?

MT I think it's a situation where you really can't talk first. You've got to be asked. There are situations when I'm called a Bible-thumper by a lot of my good friends. But *this* is one situation where I've never tried to open the conversation. I think I've just got to make my views known and leave it at that and only talk about what the gay Christian wants to talk about and just be friendly, but be quite firm on exactly what I believe myself. The other person's got to make the running. I'm quite sure about that.

There is in fact a spiritual warfare going on. We believe that the devil has deceived people, but they can't see that themselves. This has to be remembered. Then I think it's important to say that people in the Gay Christian Movement on the whole really are Christians. I think my first reaction was to say 'Oh, they obviously can't be Christians because of what they're believing', completely forgetting that I myself was a believing Christian and a practising homosexual.

On my approach to gay people who aren't Christians – I think the most important thing is to show a really positive attitude. I want to be seen and known as a Christian who's gay myself, but not a practising gay because I believe it's wrong. But I don't want to put the emphasis on the 'not practising', which is where it so often can come, but on being a Christian. A lot of the ministries to homosexuals in the States are billed up as 'ex-gay' ministries. I find that very unhelpful myself. I wouldn't call myself 'ex-gay' for a minute.

DH What would you call yourself?

MT Well, I don't want to sound pious about it, but I am a Christian first and foremost. I then have a basically homosexual orientation as well.

DH But that's subordinate?

MT Oh yes. Now, one other thing. Where some gay people

have had some involvement with the Church, they've sometimes been told that they're devil-possessed! Whilst I don't doubt that a percentage, a small percentage, of homosexuals do have homosexual problems from 'possession' – and that's quite possible – I don't think you can automatically assume that devil possession is part of the homosexual's problem. That's not so. And, therefore, some of the 'ex-gay' ministries which go on, I feel are just as harmful as the Metropolitan Community Church and the ministry that they are conducting. This, of course, is pro gay and says that gay is good.

As far as non gays in the Church are concerned, I see homophobia as the problem. Thinking about it, I've realised that homophobia is in some ways a greater problem for the Church than homosexuality, because so many Christians are suffering from homophobia. I feel that it's a great part of my own job to help Christians overcome homophobia, which just through knowing me over a length of time they do.

DH Let me now back-track. You believe, obviously, that the Lord has taken you through and over the problem of homosexuality as it's confronted you. You now would claim 'healing'. This is your vocabulary.

MT Yes, I would say so.

DH But how do you describe this 'healing'? What is it, and what is it not, in terms of your homosexual orientation.

MT For myself, I would say that I have really experienced victory over temptation. But that isn't a once for all thing. It's something that I've got to keep on claiming. I can't become smug and say, 'I'm healed', because I know that I can fall into a homosexual sin, just as easily as I can fall into plenty of other sins again. And so in saying, 'I believe the Lord's made me whole in this area', that doesn't mean he's taken away temptation. I'm still facing temptation, but I know that I *can* overcome it because I've done so time and time again; and

126

with the Lord's strength I'll go on overcoming homosexual temptations. I think the other area, which is connected, where I've really found healing, is in the complete loss of my own fear. I am not afraid of anything on the whole subject now. I'm not afraid of talking to homosexuals, I'm not afraid of being known as a homosexual, and I'm not even afraid of the temptation. It doesn't frighten me to think that the devil is going to tempt me homosexually. There is just no fear, because of my knowledge of how God accepts me as I am, and what God is doing for me as I am at the moment. I regard myself as just an ordinary Christian.

DH And where do you go from now?

MT First of all, I'm involved in a ministry called True Freedom Trust,[1] which is run by somebody who was a very active homosexual in the gay scene, until he was converted about seven years ago. He's a fellow called Martin Hallett. I'm involved with him in distributing their literature and in some counselling if anything comes up in the North East area. Then apart from that, I feel that my main role – the place where I get the most opportunity for work at the moment – is in talking to Christians about homosexuality, straight Christians, and helping them to overcome their own homophobia, which seems completely inbred in so many people. I think that's where the Lord's using me most of all at the moment. But I also go along to Durham CHE every now and again, and I really keep abreast of the gay news media.

DH Finally, can I ask you about a problem I have? I endorse everything, pretty well everything, you've said. But what about the Board for Social Responsibility's Working Party Report, in which it is now argued that there are circumstances in which a homosexual relationship is justifiable? I believe we have to say, 'No, this is very wrong.' We've got to argue heavily against this and other similar strands of theology, which come about

127

probably through good motives and a concern for love and compassion.

So we've got to say, 'No, the Working Party's arguments and conclusions are wrong.' Consequently we've got to be negative. *Yet* at the same time we've got to exercise love and sensitivity towards the homosexual. We've got to be positive. How can we do both at the same time?

MT I think that what you need is for people who are homosexuals to say all this. For myself, I know what I'm talking about, and I also know the way gay people are going to react to what's said. It will probably be taken better from someone like me.

NOTES

1 *True Freedom Trust*, provides a confidential counselling service ('Harbinger') and a teaching ministry on homosexuality for churches and individuals ('Chandler'). Phone 051-678-9961 or write to PO Box 3, Wirral, Merseyside, L49 6NY

PART III

THE CHURCH AND HOMOSEXUALITY – PASTORAL CONSIDERATIONS

DAVID WATSON

THE CHURCH AND HOMOSEXUALITY

'Things came to a head a few years ago, after a long period of hating myself, raising a fist to God, complaining "Why have you made me like this?", and experiencing the pain caused by awkwardness in relationships. There is also the guilt brought about by social unacceptance...'

These comments made to me by someone with a homosexual orientation indicate something of the loneliness, self-hatred, frustration and despair that, in varying degrees, literally millions of men and women feel in society today. To ignore such cries is to lack both responsibility and compassion. Sadly the traditional attitude of society towards homosexuals has been negative, ranging from ridicule to rejection, from disgust to active persecution. Thousands of homosexuals, for example, were 'purged' under Hitler's totalitarian regime.

'I had been teased and made fun of for many years,' wrote someone to me. 'Secondary school children, who are going through insecure stages themselves, give vent to their fears by picking on someone who epitomises all they are afraid of, or have been told to be wary of by their parents ... At this stage teasing got worse and worse for me, and because I was nervous I began to develop the sort of nervous gestures and mannerisms which others found so funny ... Teasing and ridicule for me continued right through until coming to university ... Becoming a Christian was a great source of inner comfort and strength, but I found it hard when, even at church, the one place I hoped to escape to, teasing sometimes took place...'

Homophobia

Tragically the Church has all too often adopted the social – and worldly – hostility against homosexuals. Under the cloak of righteousness it has shown little of the love and compassion of Jesus Christ. As Christians we have often been self-righteous. censorious and condemning. We have quoted texts with severity rather than sensitivity. We have preached, but not listened. We have often avoided, misunderstood and rejected the very individuals to whom Jesus always offered unjudging friendship. If there is a 'problem of homosexuality', it begins with the problem of the Church's 'homophobia' – a word invented by the gay movement for the neurotic fears and revulsion that many display towards homosexuals. God clearly has to deal with homophobia, just as he wants to bring us all into wholeness, including that powerful area of our sexuality. Therefore, as a Christian minister with a heterosexual orientation, I see the need for the Church to repent deeply for unloving, hypocritical attitudes, which both compound the frustrations and loneliness of many, and at the same time deny the grace of our Lord Jesus Christ, whose tenderness and love alone can set us all free.

A Christian with homosexual tendencies wrote to me about a Christian conference he once attended. In the light of 1 Corinthians 6:9 – the passage about homosexuals (amongst others) not inheriting the kingdom of God – someone had asked if it were right to assume that *no-one* could possibly be a homosexual *and* a Christian. 'Nothing was done to refute this. The discussion which followed was very vague, and the whole difference between "being and doing" was barely touched on. I left the meeting convinced that I wasn't a Christian. After a while I just had to sit down and work out for myself, with a Bible, that I was still a Christian – but no thanks to the Church! Others may have been there who, feeling lonely, disillusioned and confused, may well have found a welcome solace in the Gay Liberation Movement . . .' The trouble is, as the Church of England's Report on *Homosexual Relationships* rightly asserts, 'the hostility which the majority of the community may feel towards homosexuals serves to isolate and strengthen a subculture in which a person's homosexuality becomes the central fact of his existence. In one sense the homosexual subculture produces a pull towards itself as an attractive way of solving the problems of isolation. In another sense the hostility of heterosexual people provides a push which segregates homosexuals into a subculture of their own.'[1] All this simply confuses the problem, makes it harder for homosexuals to find full integration into modern society, and takes away the urgency for society itself both to change its attitudes and to accept a minority group with compassion and understanding.

Christian love

This is precisely where the Church should have something positive to offer. Jesus commands us that we should love one another as he has loved us, and his love is always an understanding love which seeks to serve the person in need. We need therefore to understand both the nature of true Christian love and the needs of those we are commanded to serve.

Christian love is both sensitive and strong. It cares for people as people, regardless of the divisive and judgemental labels we may give to one another; yet at the same time it cares deeply about the highest good of both the individual and the society in which he or she lives. The difficulty is that, with our judgement impaired by the sin of man, the 'highest good' is difficult to define. It is totally inadequate to say that love is our guide, since there are many different kinds of love. *Eros*, for example is not only sexual love; it seeks essentially for self-gratification. It is by nature selfish and therefore, by itself, can be both powerful and destructive. We often fail to love ourselves, in the highest sense of the word: what we pursue 'in love' is not always for our ultimate good. How much harder it is to be truly objective about loving someone else, unless we have some external guidelines. This is precisely where God's word in the Bible becomes so important. Here we have the Maker's Instructions. We are free to ignore them if we wish, but we are not free to ignore the consequences.

Christian love, in contrast to *eros* or *philia* (brotherly affection) is unique. There is nothing soft or indulgent about *agapē*: 'This is love . . . that God loved us and sent his Son to be the expiation for our sins.' Christian love is spelt s-a-c-r-i-f-i-c-e. There is no compassion without cost. And because God cares profoundly about our highest good – not primarily about the fulfilment of our immediate desires – he may say some things that are hard to accept. As one homosexual friend of mine has put it, 'The call to celibacy can sound so hard. Some of the things that Jesus said were very hard, but he had the love which gave him the right to say them. Too often the Church has had the correct hard words, but has not had the love with which to say those words.' Jesus spoke sharply to the self-righteous religious critics who brought to him a woman caught in the act of adultery: 'Let him who is without sin among you be the first to throw a stone at her.' Yet, although Jesus forgave the woman, refusing to condemn her, he also refused to lower the standards of God as given in the Scriptures. 'Go,' he said to her, 'and *do not sin again.*'

A vital distinction
Although a vital distinction must be made between homosexual *tendency* and homosexual *activity* ('being' is not the same as 'doing'), the Scriptures are unanimous in their assertion that homosexual acts are sinful acts. So are heterosexual acts outside marriage. It is not that one sin is worse than another; but, although God is infinite in his mercy and grace, he never compromises his standards to accommodate our human weaknesses. In *Homosexual Relationships* the Working Party states, 'Traditionally the Church has ruled out homosexual practices entirely and we are not persuaded that this was a judgement that can now be

seen as totally erroneous or of merely temporary validity, for it does follow in principle from an understanding of sexuality which we believe to be fundamentally sound and defensible. But there is one important respect in which the situation has changed. It was assumed until quite recently that every mature individual was capable of a heterosexual response. It is now clear that for a significant proportion of the population this is not the case.'[2] The last point seems true; but it is by no means clear that the biblical writers assumed that every mature individual was capable of a heterosexual response. The Board for Social Responsibility in its Critical Observations makes this point.

Homosexual activity in the first century was probably far more widespread than it is now, at least within the Gentile world. Of the first fifteen Roman Emperors, fourteen were said to be practising homosexuals. Clearly many Gentiles converted to Christ had also engaged in homosexual activities. However, when the apostle Paul wrote, 'and such were some of you. But you were washed, you were sanctified, you were justified in the name of the Lord Jesus Christ', he does not necessarily imply that their sexual orientation had changed from homo to hetero. That may well have happened to some; but *all* had been forgiven, accepted by God in Christ, and cleansed from the sin of sexual activity outside the male–female relationship of marriage. In this same passage 'some of you' refers equally to those who had been immoral and adulterers. Their sexual desires might well have been as strong as ever; but they had repented of immoral acts, received forgiveness, and were seeking to live chaste lives controlled by the Spirit of God.

Nowhere in the Bible is the homosexual tendency or urge condemned. There may have been many understandable reasons for those tendencies to have been there at all – some of which we shall see later. But in the seven passages where homosexuality is mentioned briefly (Genesis 19:1–11; Leviticus 18:22; 20:13; Judges 19:22–25; Romans 1:25–26; 1 Corinthians 6:9; 1 Timothy 1:9–10), it is never approved by

God. Instead the practice is regarded as both sinful and un-natural. It would be quite wrong to regard it as *the* sin, or one which especially incurs the judgement of God. For example, it is highly doubtful if Sodom was destroyed for this sin alone. Instead, it is *rebellion* that is regarded as serious as the sin of witchcraft (1 Samuel 15:23), and *pride* is the abomination which God hates (Proverbs 16:5). It is therefore the mocking of God by knowingly flouting his standards and by proudly revelling in the shame of sinful practices that causes the wrath of God to be revealed (see Romans 1:18–32).

Human sexuality
A fuller discussion of the biblical passages is to be found elsewhere in this book. However, it is important to start, not with the passages about homosexuality, but with the nor-mative pattern of human sexuality, as given in the opening chapters of Genesis. There, when God created man in his own image, he created male *and* female. 'Be fruitful and multiply,' he told them. The whole mystery of man and woman becoming 'one flesh' is seen, not only as a profound creation ordinance, but later as a symbol of the intimate communion between Christ and his Church. Biologically we are either male or female: that is our gender identity – we must be one or the other, with only most rare exceptions. And it is together, male and female, that we exhibit the image of God.

Since the fall of man, however, that image has been marred and our relationships spoilt. Our fellowship with God has been broken by sin; and instead of loving one another with that pure, self-giving love of God, we often use and abuse one another, sometimes hating and killing one another. In this confusion of twisted and broken relation-ships, it is not surprising that our sexual relationships also have fallen into disarray. Homosexual and heterosexual alike urgently need redemption through the grace of God. Salvation means wholeness. God wants to restore us to his image once again, so that our relationships with him and with one another can be made whole. Admittedly this process will not be completed this side of heaven; it is only then that we shall be fully like him. But if we have this hope in us we should take steps to purify ourselves – and purify our relationships – as God himself is pure.

Given man's alienation both from God and from himself, it is a great mistake to think of sexual problems as the all-important ones. As one Christian student wrote to me: 'Sex isn't the most important thing in my life. I used to relate absolutely everything to THE PROBLEM (ie homo-sexuality). But as I've learnt that there are other areas that need sorting out, I've had less trouble.' Another said: 'If someone is homosexual, nine times out of ten that is one of a whole host of closely associated but different problems and neuroses, hang-ups and tensions.' That of course is true, as can be seen from the complex and varied causes that may lead to homosexuality. At the beginning of this part of the book I have quoted someone who used to raise a fist to God, complaining bitterly, 'Why have you made me like this?' The same cry could come from anyone with any physical, mental or emotional maladjustment. There are no easy answers. We all live in a fallen imperfect world in which creation itself is groaning and waiting for redemption. Immunity from suffering is not guaranteed for anyone; nor can we rightly ask the question once raised about a man born blind, 'Who sinned, this man or his parents?' In answer to this, Jesus replied that it was neither this man nor his parents, but that God had allowed the condition in order that 'the works of God might be made manifest in him'. We shall see later some of the ways in which every human situation can be turned to the glory of God. It is often in our pains and sorrows that God is doing something especially significant in our lives.

Causes of homosexuality
If we are to love one another with understanding, some

137

insight into the causes of homosexuality *may* be helpful, although the debate has often been complex and confusing. Abnormalities in family life seem a major cause: for example 'a domineering mother and a passive, ineffectual father', according to some analytical theories.[3] Others have suggested a biological explanation; and although research has failed to confirm a theory of genetic abnormality, there are some indications that hormonal factors may contribute to homosexual orientation. Loneliness will obviously create its own problems in terms of relationships, and one man told me that 'a lot of homosexuals have been as starved of the right sort of love and affection' that, when they do find it they often have a desire 'to smother, to be possessive'. The same, of course, can be equally true of heterosexuals. Others feel inadequate sexually in their formative teenage years, partly due to television hero-figures who exaggerate their sexuality, and partly due to the social pressures that are everywhere today. Especially unhelpful is the widespread assumption that love equals sex, and that the answer to loneliness is some sort of sexual activity. Such false and shallow assumptions in turn breed enormous frustrations and bitterness, and only add to the sense of guilt and alienation. Nevertheless, activities which bring temporary pleasure soon become habits, and habits soon shape behaviour. It is then that changes become much more difficult.

For the purposes of this particular section I am concerned not primarily with the causes (one person told me that he found discussion of the causes very unhelpful and negative), but with the positive and constructive issues that can be raised.

Identity
Probably the most important factor is the whole question of personal identity. The label 'a homosexual' can be quite devastating and crippling in its effect on any individual. In the context of a book such as this the expression may perhaps be used legitimately; but no man or woman should

138

express their true identity in terms of their sexuality. I am not 'a homosexual' or 'a heterosexual'. I am a human being made in the image of God. By faith in Jesus Christ I am also a son of God, indwelt by the Spirit of God. And I have numerous Christian brothers or sisters whom I am not to think of primarily in terms of their sexuality. A friend of mine, and a brother in Christ, was first considerably helped when a wise counsellor said to him: 'Don't dare label yourself! You're not "a homosexual". You're not "an anything". You are a son of God. That is the very start and end of your identity. Everything else is merely secondary – a characteristic which may have its problems. But your identity – who you are – is a child of God.'

Numerous people today face an identity crisis: they do not know who they are or where they belong. Hence a label like 'homosexual' (or 'big nose', 'flat feet', 'pot belly', alcoholic, asthmatic, diabetic, etc) can so easily, as a label, become a factor which causes great loneliness and destroys self-respect. Someone wrote to me, 'The big breakthrough was when I stopped thinking of myself as "a homosexual". How can a child of God call himself something like that?' Another person put it like this: 'How does God see you? Does he see you as some hateful object that he finds an abomination, or does he see you as his son whom he delights in? When I began to understand that God loved me with that sort of love, I began to love myself with an appropriate sort of love. The key comes in realising that you *are* a child of God, and that you *are* the object of the most incredible love directly from God.' When anyone begins to discover his true identity in these terms, it is not long before he (or she) begins to experience the fulness of life that God longs for us to enjoy, whatever our personal handicaps or situation may be.

In his helpful book, *Eros Defiled*, Dr John White writes, 'The deepest longing in the heart of a homosexual is the longing all of us experience, the longing to be known, to be loved and to be accepted just as we are and for always.

Eroticism may be important to the homosexual, but it is no more important to him or her than to anyone else. It has precisely the same function as in all of us: that of a pathway to the end of aloneness.'[4] Yet the real end of aloneness comes when we love and accept people as people, each one of infinite value to a Creator God, each one through Christ a potential member of God's eternal family. Accepting an individual is not necessarily the same as approving his or her lifestyle and behaviour. There are many factors in each one of us that God may want to change or control. At the same time he loves us just as we are, and calls us to do the same towards one another. Roger Moss[5] suggests that instead of the false but common assumption

Homosexual = Immoral = Undesirable

a more constructive Christian attitude should be

Homosexual = Person = Qualifying for love

In this sense, at any rate, the Christian too will call for 'homosexual equality', even if he disagrees with some of the other aims of the Campaign which bears this name.

Healing or change

How far should those with homosexual tendencies look for healing, perhaps a complete change of sexual orientation? Christian counsellors with gifts in what is often termed 'inner healing' have written about the remarkable changes taking place when a man or woman experiences the healing power of Christ in some area where there have been deep hurts in the past. It is sometimes through such hurts perhaps at a formative period of a person's sexuality, that homosexual tendencies have developed. Through prayer it is possible to take the Spirit of Christ back to those emotional wounds, to bring new release and wholeness to the individual concerned. It would be wrong, however, to suggest that such healing is automatically available to everyone.

140

Certainly remarkable changes of many kinds have been wrought by the power of the risen Christ, and his grace is clearly promised as being sufficient for us, whatever problems we may have to battle with, sometimes persistently so. But he does not automatically take away what may well seem to us to be a painful thorn in the flesh. In the whole area of healing we must bow to the sovereignty and wisdom of God; only then can we discover the other 'riches of his grace' that he has planned for us. We have to accept the fact that many have prayed for healing from homosexuality but do not appear to have received it in any obvious way.

Many homosexuals would object to the idea that homosexuality is a 'sickness'. It is, they say, simply 'a variant in sexual development', and therefore the whole question of 'healing' or 'cure' is inappropriate. I can understand that. But if we accept the clear biblical principle that sexual activities of any kind between two persons outside the marriage bond are not right in the sight of God, the question still remains as to whether or not homosexual orientation can be changed. Much depends on whether or not the person concerned wants to change. Many do not. They resent the implications that they are sick, needing some form of treatment. Equally, others reject the statement that homosexual acts are sinful acts, 'since God has made us this way'. In any case the call to repentance and to radical changes in patterns of behaviour is too threatening and painful for many to consider. Yet it is only when we face up to such challenges in many areas of our life that the possibility of freedom becomes real.

We shall return to this matter of repentance and forgiveness later. For those who sincerely want to change there are various techniques in modern psychiatry available, and some of them can be of some help to some people with homosexual orientation. That is probably all that can in fairness be said at this present time. Dr John White, Associate Professor of Psychiatry at the University of Manitoba, describes several of these techniques in *Eros Defiled*,[6] but is

141

cautious about both the claims and the morality of certain forms of treatment. In common with most questions of change in terms of human behaviour, a balanced view is important. For some, dramatic changes may come directly through the power of the Spirit of Christ or through the ministry of inner healing. For others, medical or psychiatric skills have performed wonders. Probably for most, there may be a bit of both, and neither the one nor the other should be ruled out of court. Even then, so much depends on the willingness for change and the ability to accept with patience problems and difficulties which doggedly persist.

Let those who have personally battled with such problems speak for themselves. 'When I was first converted all homosexual feelings seemed virtually to go, but then I had been a very promiscuous homosexual, my life was completely sex-orientated. I didn't have any hang-ups or guilt feelings. I was quite happy. I didn't really want to change. But then the Lord broke into my life and he changed me ... But after three years as a Christian, I had become so narrow-minded and so insensitive in my relationship with other Christians who were experiencing sexual problems, I just could not identify with them. I thought, why can't they claim the victory that God has given to me? Then, after three years, I suddenly became aware of homosexual feelings again. At first it hit me, like a sort of anti-conversion experience. I wondered what was happening. But then I suddenly realised that my whole attitude towards people experiencing difficulties changed dramatically. I was now able to identify with them and understand them. Now I see all this as being a part of my healing as a Christian.'

Another man who knows that God has given him healing and deliverance from homosexual problems admits that this does not mean that he no longer has homosexual attractions. 'I don't think we are responsible for every thought and feeling that comes our way, but we are responsible for what we do with it. I tend to make my sexual identity a celebration of God's gift to me. There are many people who

142

are trying to pretend they are not attracted to the opposite sex – or the same sex – and they end up with problems. What I do is to recognise it as a sin and put it behind me. No matter how much a woman is pestered by a man, she cannot bring forth a child unless she conceives. And no matter how much we may be pestered by temptation, we cannot bring forth sin unless it conceives in us.'[7]

It is here that the Christian needs to claim the power of Christ over temptation, providing he is not leading himself foolishly into temptation. However, it is when we humbly acknowledge our personal weakness and inability to manage in our own strength that we can most of all experience the grace of God. The problem may not disappear; it could even continue as fiercely as ever. But if, through it all, we are made to be consciously and continuously dependent upon God for his strength and forgiveness, God has graciously brought us to the place where we are meant to be all the time anyway. 'Without me you can do nothing.' Often it is only in our felt weakness that we really know that to be true.

Repentance and forgiveness
Whatever our orientation may be, all of us need to surrender our sexuality to God, so that he may be fully in control of that powerful gift he has given us – a gift that can be so creative or so destructive. Further, if in any area our sexuality is not honouring to God, the path to new release and freedom is always through repentance.

'Repentance is the moral and spiritual mechanism by which we lay hold of the healing, reintegrating work of God in Jesus Christ, his work of restoring to human identity its image of intended godliness. In regard to homosexuality, the most important witness of Scripture is not condemnation but the promise of liberation ... and Christian freedom is never licence to live as before (Galatians 5:13). It is the gift of power to have done with alienating, guilt-inducing behaviour. This is the freedom of inner harmony and healing, accomplished again and again as persons are open in penitence and resolve. Repentance means the decision to be personally responsible for choices. It is the refusal to drift, the refusal to delay. And this refusal rests on a critical prior decision which is the *refusal to pass the buck*.'[8]

This latter point is of immense importance. Frustrations and resentments grow in intensity when we abdicate personal responsibility and blame others, maybe God himself, for our present problems. Where there is no personal responsibility there is no personal significance. We become a poor piece of flotsam and jetsam tossed around on the turbulent seas of heredity and environment. However, although we may not always be responsible for our situation, we are responsible for our reactions to our situation. I once talked with a woman who had been classified as a 'chronic schizophrenic'. There seemed no hope for her apart from indefinite hospitalisation. All the counselling sessions brought her back to a traumatic event when, at the age of five or six, she had been raped. Here was an emotional giant in the past that could not be removed. One Christian counsellor, however, said to her, 'You are full of self-pity, and unless you repent of your self-pity you will never be healed.' The woman was furious. Why should *she* have to repent when she had been the tragic victim of a sexual assault? Slowly the truth about her own responsibility for her present attitudes dawned on her. She began to repent. Within a year she was completely healed. When I last heard of her, she was a Christian missionary serving Christ in a remote and difficult part of his world. Accepting her responsibility led to repentance; and this in turn brought her both significance, freedom and a new life altogether.

It is here that the Church, in its compassionate swing away from self-righteous judgements, can become thoroughly confused concerning God's self-revealed standards. One practising homosexual admitted later, having repented of his sinful behaviour, 'the last thing I wanted' was for Christians to 'condone what I was doing'. When there are no clear moral signposts we can be hopelessly lost in the fog of moral uncertainty. I spent a long evening once with a local group of the Campaign for Homosexual Equality. They had asked me to speak on some such subject as 'Homosexuality and the Christian Faith', and then to open it up for discussion. What depressed me about the evening was that most if not all of them wanted only one thing from me: to endorse all homosexual practices – 'gay is good'. But this I could not do, because 'my conscience is captive to the word of God'. Although I tried to be as gentle and as understanding as I knew how, the discussion generated much anger and bitterness; and I came away extremely sad.

It is certainly no gospel to tell a practising homosexual to 'stop it' or to 'change your way of life'. In his own strength he cannot do this. On almost every moral issue, 'I can will what is right, but I cannot do it' (Romans 7:18). God's law brings freedom to no-one. But as soon as we acknowledge that we are living contrary to God's law, the first clear word from God is for us to *repent*. And that repentance refers not only to specific sins (though that is important). We need to repent of our whole attitude of rebellion towards God, which lies behind all sin. It is when we confess humbly that our whole attitude to God has been wrong, come to the Cross of Christ for his forgiveness, and receive the life and power of his Spirit within us, that we begin to find true peace and freedom, together with the possibility of change – or at least the ability to overcome the pressures and temptations which can so easily lead us back into moral and spiritual bondage. That is just what the apostle Paul meant when he wrote, 'Some of you were like that. But you have been purified from sin: you have been dedicated to God: you have been put right with God by the Lord Jesus Christ and by the Spirit of our God' (1 Corinthians 6:11, GNB).

'Thus the gay person is joined to a forgiving, redemptive, loving, truthful, and yes, disciplining body of believers. It is here that he receives the hope and the power to be changed ... In counselling homosexuals I have encountered two

145

primary tasks. The first is to help the homosexual understand grace. God's forgiveness is free; it is also unqualified and unconditional. Many homosexuals come to Christ carrying a great load of guilt. Many will struggle with failure in their Christian lives. For them the gospel must be preached in authority and power. Christ forgives! He forgives freely! If we try to atone for our own sins, then we diminish the work of Christ. The second task is to offer hope to the Christian homosexual. The Christian community is to be a community of hope ... Here there will be warmth, openness, and the absence of threat. Here the individual will find a new family of brothers and sisters in Christ. Their word to each other is always a word of hope. Sin does not have the last word: only Christ does – and our hope is to be conformed to him.'[9]

One young man wrote to me to explain what had especially helped him. 'I realised that in God's eyes I'm clean, and that through him I can cope and overcome. I believed this in faith until it became a reality.' Moreover, just as God loves, forgives and accepts each one of us, warts and all, so we are called to do precisely the same to one another. In fact the *experience* of God's love will come to many people only when it is clearly and tangibly expressed through other Christians. It is never easy both recognising sin as sin, and at the same time genuinely loving and accepting the sinner. But that is what the pure love of God is all about; and his grace within us will enable us to care for one another in this sensitive and honest way.

Relationships of love in Christ

Some of the problems and tensions surrounding sexual relationships (of all kinds) have arisen from the failure of the Church to become, in any meaningful sense, the true body of Christ, or the loving family of God. Gentile society of the first century was notoriously permissive and immoral; but although there were some tragic moral lapses within the Church (such as at Corinth), stable and caring relationships

146

were able to develop in a remarkable way because of the strength and depth of the brother–sister relationship. Those first Christians learnt to be as committed to one another as they were to Christ. They took seriously Christ's new commandment to love one another with a love that was marked not by eroticism but by service. In this atmosphere of genuine caring and sharing the emotional needs of both men and women were largely fulfilled and stabilised.

Martin Hallett of *True Freedom Trust* has put it in this way: 'We all have emotional needs. We really desire to love and be loved. I believe that God wants to meet those needs, not only through the Lord Jesus himself, but through relationships with other Christians. This is desperately important, because if we are not emotionally fulfilled, our erotic sexuality will come as an attempt to meet those emotional needs. If you look in the adverts of *Gay News* you will see that nearly all homosexuals are in some way looking for a stable, permanent relationship (as most people are), and this is something that the Lord Jesus wants to meet. Therefore fulfilling relationships with other Christians are very important. When we are open to God's Spirit, we can learn to lay down our lives for one another, and to be open and honest with each other. If emotional needs are being met in this way in the Church, sexual problems and frustrations, whatever they happen to be, will be far less difficult to deal with.'[10]

Sexual activities should never be the most important aspect of any person's life. In its rightful context (marriage) sex can be a beautiful expression of something that is much more profound and lasting: a deep bond of tender and self-giving love. The finest quality of such love is what God offers us in Jesus Christ; and therefore the Spirit of God wants to create between true Christians a richness of relationships that can, to a large extent at least, satisfy the deep longings in the heart of all of us, including those for whom marriage (for various reasons) is not a possibility. It is also quite misleading to assume that marriage, with all its

147

legitimate sexual activities, automatically fulfils our hunger for love. No one person can, or should, fulfil all the emotional needs of another person. That is why God brings us into his greater family, where we can find and develop deeply satisfying relationships of love – God's *agapē* love – on the brother–sister basis. Marriage is not meant to provide us with the wealth of such love, otherwise there would be little 'good news' of Jesus Christ for the single, divorced, widow and widower, let alone those with homosexual orientation. It is said sometimes that marriage is like a besieged city: all those outside want to get in, and all those inside want to get out! That may be a somewhat cynical attitude, but it certainly indicates that marriage is not necessarily the ultimate in terms of deeply loving relationships.

The development of the Church as a caring community of love is one of the most urgent necessities of this present time, when society as a whole is littered with the breakdown of relationships at every level. It is when the Church can demonstrate that it is a new society in Christ that it has something to say to a world that is falling apart. One Christian homosexual wrote to me of the 'incredible support' he received from the deep relationships formed through the house fellowship in his home church. 'In the end I think it is the love and support of people who do not know of my problem that has been the most helpful. It is so easy to make *it* (the homosexuality) the centre of everything.' Another man spoke of the sustaining strength of his Christian community in this way: 'The great security for me is that there are half a dozen men who know absolutely everything about me, which means I don't have to pretend any more.'[11] Another person told me: 'I have been surrounded by many people that have been so good, so loving, so accepting and so understanding; and it is tragic that others are surrounded by so much misunderstanding, so little acceptance, so much hostility.'

The real tragedy is that such rejection can often come from within the Church. Although I believe it is right to

148

reject homosexual practices, it is both hypocritical and judgemental to reject the individual concerned. It seems that many of us in the Church do not realise how many are crying out for love; or, if we do, we may not admit it for fear of the pain and hurts which will certainly come when we really open ourselves up to one another, thereby making ourselves vulnerable. Yet when out of love for Jesus we are willing to do this, the Spirit of God can work through us to bring immense liberation to others. One homosexual spoke of the 'tremendous relief' of belonging to such a caring group. Another talked of being 'much more emotionally secure and at ease' now that he had found true brothers and sisters in Christ. He acknowledged that his sexual frustrations had become far less than when he was lonely and unloved. Of course!

Dr Frank Lake has often commented that, through the cultural inhibitions of certain societies (such as the British) where the tenderness of human touch is usually denied between friends (especially of the same sex), the consequences are either the agonies of emotional alienation or the passions of sexual activities. 'There are so many in authority, making pronouncements about human life and the nature of loving, who have never been able to visit, even for a day's excursion, the world of real people with real bodies and real relationships. They live shut away in their minds, outside their bodies, unaware of the sensations and feelings that provide the basis for the "one-flesh" mystery . . . They are people who were driven by the trauma of birth to split off the mind from the crushed and tortured body. They jettisoned their bodies at birth as part of the evil world of mother, flesh, guts, genitals, women and embodied men. They have taken refuge in an ivory tower of mental and "spiritual" superiority. In New Testament times they would be called gnostics. Their secret scorn of bodily intimacies of all human relationships, whether with men or women, is an even deeper and more drastic injury to the line of love and trust than yours [referring to homosexuals] . . . So, my

149

friend, beware of those who would counsel you from the homophile clubs to become non-sexual, but beware equally of those churchmen who would counsel you out of the aridities of their schizoid fear of all the bodily life of touching and tender loving holding. They choose to forget John, lying on Jesus' bosom at the great meal.'[12]

To achieve deep loving relationships in Christ is never easy. In fact, without him it is impossible, because we do not naturally have that capacity of love. Essentially it is the love of God alone that can create the healing atmosphere of a caring fellowship in which we can all grow up into full maturity in Christ. A Christian leader once asked me, 'Have you come to that point in your relationships where you *have* to depend on the Holy Spirit?' At the time we were finding close relationships 'heavy' and difficult. But God's grace can enable us to create the true biblical concept of fellowship, defined by Ronald J. Sider as 'unconditional availability to and unlimited liability for the other brothers and sisters – emotionally, financially, and spiritually'.[13]

A fulfilled life
The fulfilment of any life depends to a large extent on the aims of that life. Are those aims in tune with the ultimate purpose of life, as God has revealed it to us in Jesus Christ? There are numerous healthy, wealthy, married and successful people who frankly are lost when it comes to any clear sense of direction in life. For them fulfilment will always be a problem, whatever their sexuality, prosperity or achievement.

Jesus taught clearly that the basic purpose of life is to know God, and that the primary aim is to seek first his kingdom. If, however, we see *ourselves* at the centre of the universe, with God (if he exists at all) justifying his existence by giving us all an equal chance to satisfaction and happiness here on earth, we shall often be fraught with frustrations. We are not at the centre of everything. God is. And when we make it our aim to please him, in the midst of a world that is

150

full of sin and pain and suffering, that can transform our whole attitude to life. 'The chief end of man is to glorify God and to enjoy him for ever.' It is when we seek first to glorify God that we can begin to enjoy him and to know the fulness of joy that ultimately comes from being continuously in his presence. Jesus never married. He formed deep and pure relationships of love with other men and women. He was often misunderstood, despised, rejected, persecuted and finally crucified. Yet, because it was always his foremost aim to please his Father in heaven, he clearly possessed a fullness of life and joy that made him so immensely attractive to ordinary and often needy people. His sufferings, which on the Cross were beyond anything we shall ever have to experience, were truly 'innocent sufferings'; but by accepting his Father's will and by living to his Father's glory he lived the only perfect life this world has ever known. Missing out on certain pleasurable experiences and knowing pain and loneliness are no impassable barriers to a life of genuine fulfilment. It is largely a question of ultimate aims and purposes.

In many respects a homosexual who accepts God's standards about sex is in the same position as numerous heterosexuals for whom marriage is not possible. It is often argued that, in theory, the heterosexual at least has the option. But in practice that option, for countless thousands of people and for different reasons, is simply not there. Once that situation is accepted, however, the Spirit of God is able to lift that person out of the natural human reactions of anger, bitterness or despair, into tremendous qualities of compassion, gentleness, sensitivity and selflessness. Far from becoming less than fully human, such persons, filled with the Spirit of God, can discover an abundance of life that many 'normal' people never find.

One man who had clearly experienced the truth of all this at some depth said to me, 'Whereas I used to be ... cursing God for my homosexuality, and resenting it ("What a life of misery you have condemned me to!"), now I can say, "Well, thank you God because you have shown me so much and given me so much through it." Ultimately the homosexual finds it no harder, no easier, than any single person who has his or her own frustrations and desires to deal with. But there are a lot of hang-ups and labels to be cleared out of the way first before he can realise that. Then he can start to learn what God means by living in a family.'

In one sense it could be said that a person with homosexual tendencies *is* worse off than a man or woman who is (or can be) happily married. But if we start comparing ourselves with others, in almost any area of human fortune or misfortune, we shall very quickly find ourselves trapped in the deceptive snare of self-pity, with all the associated evils that go with it. At the time of writing I have suffered on and off for fourteen years from quite bad asthma. In many ways it has been a handicap, and has restricted my movements. But how foolish if I had indulged in self-pity over this! Of course I should like to be free from asthma. But thankfully I *am* free from countless worse problems that others have to face, and I have also learnt so much from God in the midst of difficult and trying circumstances. I would not have chosen this slight affliction for myself, but I can at least see how God has graciously used it to enrich my experience of his love; he has given me much greater understanding and compassion towards those battling with similar or other problems; he has reminded me of my own frailty and of my need to look to him for life and breath and everything. And for all these things I can really praise him.

Every area of personal need is an opportunity for us to learn more of 'the unsearchable riches of Christ'. 'For we have not a high priest who is unable to sympathise with our weaknesses, but one who in every respect has been tempted as we are, yet without sin' (Hebrews 4:15). This is an astonishing statement! Since Jesus became fully human, it is surely certain that he felt the pressures of sexual temptations, perhaps homosexual temptations. The Gospel records are silent on these specific details; but since Jesus fully entered into our humanity, he fully understands the weaknesses of our humanity. Not only that, for as often as we come to him we 'receive mercy and find grace to help in time of need'. As we try to obey and honour Christ in every area of our lives there may be times of pain and loneliness, perhaps even deep depression following the necessary breaking-off of a wrong relationship. But in these ways we may discover as never before the reality and comfort of the love of Christ – a love poured into our hearts by his Spirit, and expressed tenderly towards us by our brothers and sisters in Christ.

It is only in this way that we are really able to help others. The apostle Paul, experiencing endless hurts and pains, hunger and loneliness, rejection and persecution, was still able to burst out frequently into thanksgiving to 'the merciful Father, the God from whom all help comes! He helps us in all our troubles, so that we are able to help others who have all kinds of troubles, using the same help that we ourselves have received from God' (2 Corinthians 1:3-4).

One man who has battled through many of his difficulties raised by his homosexuality into a place of peace wrote to me in this way: 'God can use my experience to help others with the same problems. There's a whole lot of suffering in the world today, and, considering I'm healthy, have enough to eat, friends to love me, and the right number of arms, legs, fingers and toes, I really don't think that being homosexual is so terrible (well, occasionally I do!). Please God, I never will practise my homosexuality. I must hope that as time goes on I can learn how to live my life in a way that is as glorifying to God as possible as a single person.'

Does all this sound rather hard and cold, a life marked by joyless determination? One Christian homosexual admitted that it might seem like that to those who have never really known the love of Christ. But 'you will discover the richness of what you can be given by God *if only you will allow him to work*. For many Christians it seems to be "grit your teeth" and "knuckle down to it" in trying to cope with their

153

homosexual problems. They need to be touched with the love and grace of our Father in heaven. For the last two years God has made my life very full and very glad.'

Postscript for the Church

The one factor more than any other that has helped those with a homosexual orientation to come to terms with God's pattern for our lives has been the existence of a loving, accepting fellowship in Christ. Sadly not every church demonstrates this. More often we are quick to speak and slow to listen, sharp to criticise and slack to show compassion. It is here that we need seriously to repent: repent of our self-righteousness, repent of our lovelessness, repent of our homophobia, repent of compounding a problem instead of bringing freedom to those battling with it. Especially we need to discover what true Christian community is all about, in terms of strong brother–sister relationships, where many emotional needs can be fulfilled.

'I am absolutely convinced,' writes Don Williams, 'that we have not begun to see what God can do through the Church in bringing gay people to himself and giving them a new sexual identity. We have not seen this because we do not welcome the witness of many homosexual Christians who, in Christ, *have* been changed in their sexual orientation to become heterosexual.'[14]

We have to accept, however, that for many their sexual orientation does not seem to change, even if they genuinely want this. What can be said for them? 'I long to see the day when more Christian homosexuals are loved and encouraged by the fellowship to take positions of responsibility ... In this way there can be a real witness to the non-Christian gay community. This must come from homosexuals within the Church who know the true answer that Jesus can give to the whole question of homosexuality. Christians must repent of their homophobia, and gay Christians must come to know the truth. I believe that they will do so if more homosexuals are prepared to stand up and be

154

counted for Christ, to let people see what God can do in their lives, and to show that they can live a fulfilling life in Christ.'[15]

The Church, as the body of Christ, has sometimes been described as 'God with skin on'. What many people need today is 'God with skin on' to put an arm round them, to love them tenderly in a tangible way, and to offer them a shoulder to cry on. 'I long to see the Church as a glorious manifestation of the body of Christ, so the people, including homosexuals, will see the wonderful new life that the Lord Jesus offers, and his answer to all their problems, displayed through his people.'[16] When the Church lacks this visible expression of the love of God, it degenerates into verbal moralising, or, even worse, into compromising God's righteousness and condoning man's sinfulness. In this respect, when a semi-official report by the Church of England says that some homosexual relationships are justified, distress and confusion are caused all round. Nothing can be more depressing for the Christian homosexual who is courageously and painfully seeking to honour God in all his or her relationships. And nothing can be ultimately more unhelpful for the non-Christian homosexual who is looking for genuine freedom and fulfilment in life. The Maker knows what he is doing when he gives us his instructions. They are seldom easy, but he offers us the grace we need to find his highest good for our lives. If we are to be faithful to him we must adhere to his instructions and demonstrate his grace. That is God's call to the Church today.

NOTES

1 *Homosexual Relationships* (CIO: 1979) p 11, para 23
2 Ibid p 51, para 164
3 John White, *Eros Defiled* (Inter-Varsity Press, Leicester: 1978) p 114
4 Ibid p 119

5 Roger Moss, *Christians and Homosexuality* (Paternoster Press, Exeter: 1977) p 46

6 John White, op cit, pp 121–27

7 *Crusade* magazine, July 1977, p 27

8 Bishop Bennett Sims, *New Covenant* magazine, October 1978, pp 11–12

9 Don Williams, *The Bond that Breaks: will Homosexuality split the Church?* (Los Angeles: 1978) pp 125–26

10 Martin Hallett, a talk given at the Greenbelt Festival, 1979

11 Quotation from Roger Moss, op cit, p 41

12 Frank Lake, *Renewal* magazine, April–May 1976 p 26

13 Ronald J. Sider, *Rich Christians in an Age of Hunger* (Hodder & Stoughton, London: 1977) p 164

14 Don Williams, op cit, p 126

15 Martin Hallett, Greenbelt Festival, 1979

16 Martin Hallett, *Life of Faith* magazine, March 1978

Also in Hodder Christian Paperbacks

Michael Green

I BELIEVE IN THE HOLY SPIRIT

'Whilst trying to present as fully and as clearly as space and my understanding allow, the teaching of the Scriptures about the Holy Spirit,' writes Michael Green, 'I should also have been failing to meet the aims of the series if I had not had a good deal to say about the issues of the baptism, the gifts, and the fullness of the Holy Spirit . . .'

'Outstandingly clear and helpful . . . superb.' – David Watson, *Church of England Newspaper*

Canon Michael Green is the former Principal of St. John's College, Nottingham, and Rector of St. Aldgate's, Oxford.

Michael Green

WHY BOTHER WITH JESUS?

By the author of You Must Be Joking *and* I Believe in the Holy Spirit.

'Why bother?' considers Michael Green, is a widespread disease among developed nations. Nothing seems to matter any more so long as we have our rise in wages, so long as the cost of beer and cigarettes is not too high, so long as we have a colour telly.

The disease has overtaken industrial life. One by one the skilled craftsmen have been dying out: the pride in work has gone. It has affected family life: politicians talk about increased standards of living, but the television has pushed out conversation, family amusements; parents find it easier to give expensive toys rather than their time and interest; the number of divorces and maladjusted children is on the increase.

The disease has taken hold of our concern for the truth. When matters of right and wrong are settled by head-count rather than principle, a moral collapse could well be in the offing.

From this grim diagnosis Michael Green asks 'Why Bother with Jesus?', looking in detail at the qualities in Jesus which make us want to learn more about him, showing how we should 'Bother because of his claims', 'Bother because he conquered death', and 'Bother because he can change your life'.

David Watson

IS ANYONE THERE?

How can we find God?

> As I was walking up the stair
> I met a man who wasn't there.
> He wasn't there again today.
> I wish, I wish he'd stay away.

(*Hughes Mearns*)

'One half of us,' says David Watson, 'finds it difficult to believe in God because of the cynical and sceptical age in which we live, but the other half is intrigued by the possibility that he really might exist.'

In our frightening world, many are gripped by loneliness and despair. Every morning there are 210,000 extra mouths to feed. Forty nations now have nuclear power, and one strategic missile has fifteen times the explosive power of all the bombs that fell in World War II.

In the light of these global threats to our very existence, it is hardly surprising that the individual is so often crippled by a feeling of total insignificance. People turn today to all kinds of 'spiritual' solutions. 'Without God, life is extraordinarily bleak,' comments David Watson. 'If God is dead, man is dead ... on the other hand, if there is a God the picture changes dramatically. If there is a God who made us, who loves us, who has a purpose for our lives, who is ultimately in control of this world in spite of the mess we have made, and can give real answers to the questions of life and death, man's whole outlook is transformed.'

Is Anyone There? explores the answers offered by the Christian faith. David Watson, one of Britain's best known preachers and Christian writers, supports his arguments with telling examples, and line drawings illustrate his text. This book for evangelism and mission states the Christian faith in contemporary terms. David Watson is author of *One in the Spirit, I Believe in Evangelism* and *I Believe in the Church*.

David Watson

I BELIEVE IN EVANGELISM

The revolutionary story of the Rev. David Watson's ministry in York has captured the attention of press and television. Internationally renowned as an evangelist, he has been described as one of Britain's finest preachers. From his experience in a parish church, from university missions at home and overseas, he has written this major volume on evangelism which reveals the passionate convictions which motivate his ministry.

'Fresh, lively and enjoyable ... solid thinking and practical application.' – *Baptist Times*

'Extremely important ... well written and cogently argued.' – *Bishop Cuthbert Bardsley*